Bill Barnes
11/1/83

Opening
Blind Eyes

JOURNEYS IN FAITH

Opening
Blind Eyes

John R. Claypool

Journeys in Faith
Robert A. Raines, Editor

ABINGDON PRESS
Nashville

OPENING BLIND EYES

Copyright © 1983 by Abingdon Press

Library of Congress Cataloging in Publication Data

CLAYPOOL, JOHN.
  Opening blind eyes.
  (Journeys in faith)
  1. Claypool, John. 2. Baptists—United States—
Clergy—Biography. 3. Southern Baptist Convention—
Clergy—Biography. 4. Christian life—Baptist authors.
I. Title. II. Series.
  BX6495.C556A3   1983   286'.132'0924   [B]   83-11924

ISBN 0-687-29213-1

MANUFACTURED BY THE PARTHENON PRESS AT
NASHVILLE, TENNESSEE, UNITED STATES OF AMERICA

To my dearest Ann,
whose love, honesty, and encouragement
are a joy to me
and
the best enablement
I have ever known

Contents

Editor's Foreword

John Claypool tells the story of his conversion from a preoccupation with self-esteem to a concern for the whole creation. Burdened, like the typical American male, with the need to succeed, Claypool "made it" at a relatively early age: He became senior minister of a church with five thousand members. But success was not all it was cracked up to be. After a long period of dissatisfaction and inner turmoil, Claypool did a remarkable thing. He *chose* to move to a church of 450 members.

Why a choice for downward mobility at a critical time in his career? This book describes part of the reason: Claypool moved from a spirit of acquisition to one of awareness—from justification by works, as a workaholic, to the acceptance of grace, as a valuable person in God's creation.

Parallel to this conversion was another—from the personal piety of his Southern Baptist heritage to a concern for social justice. Claypool suggests that Jesus was, in his own way, a revolutionary, and in the last chapters of this book, he sketches out some of the humane revolutions in which he believes the church of Christ must be involved today.

The mode of the book is confessional. Claypool comes through as a warm human being—vulnerable, and therefore accessible to the reader. This book will be a useful meditational reflection for readers who are seeking their own quiet transformation from living by works to living by faith, from preoccupation with personal piety to participation in healing creation.

Robert A. Raines

Opening
Blind Eyes

There are many people who have sought light and truth, but they look for it outside themselves, where it is not.
                                                                    —*Augustine*

Author's Introduction

Often, the reason something has come about is as significant as its final outcome. I would like to share with you several things about the process that produced this book.

The first draft of the manuscript was written during the summer and fall of 1980. Before the final work was completed, however, my marriage, which had been troubled for several years, ended in divorce, despite honest efforts to save it. Needless to say, that grief process consumed most of my energies during the summer of 1981 and pulled me away from this project.

You will find no specific references to the end of that marriage in this book. I would have been most willing to share the knowledge gained both during that traumatic process and in the grace-filled recovery period (as I did years ago after our daughter's death) by writing about it and by talking with others who had had similar experiences. But my former spouse felt differently. She requested that I not write or speak publicly about our marriage or the death of it, and in deference to her need for that privacy, I agreed.

I can, however, affirm the grace that sustained me through that agony and that has given me new life beyond all my fondest hopes. I now have new reasons for believing in the Resurrection. There is life beyond those times when we come to the end of our human resources, times when we must say, "If there is anything more, it is up to God."

During that summer, I moved alone from Jackson, Mississippi, to New Orleans, Louisiana, to begin a year-long residency in clinical pastoral education at Southern Baptist Hospital. I also chose to continue a process of personal therapy in order to encourage and sustain a commitment to continued growth.

Then almost immediately, events began to happen which made it clear to me that God was still lovingly concerned and had work for me to do. Dr. Myron Madden, director of pastoral services at Southern Baptist Hospital; Dr. Robert E. Pearce, my supervisor; and Dr. Richard Dawes, my therapist—each played an important role in calling me back to abundant life and wholeness. And best of all, God soon brought Ann Williams into my life.

Ann had been brought to New Orleans after she had sustained multiple skull fractures in a near-fatal fall, and her brokenness of body and my brokenness of spirit were to become the raw material of a new creation for both of us. We were married in the summer of 1982 and moved to Lubbock, Texas, where I joined the pastoral team at Second Baptist Church. This has been "the land of beginning again"—a place where we have been able to serve and share together. Thus "the worst of times" paved the way for "the best of times," and in an atmosphere of grace and gratitude, this manuscript was picked up again and completed.

I owe abundant thanks to many helpers along the way. Pat Travis, in Jackson, typed the original draft and was a comfort and source of strength during my last days at Northminster Baptist Church. Here in Lubbock, Gloria Gaines has worked long and tirelessly. Most of all, my dear Ann has provided both encouragement and support in this most recent segment of my journey. Whatever good may come of these words is our gift to you.

John R. Claypool

PART ONE: LOOKING BACK

1

In the Beginning

I was intrigued by the questions that set in motion this series of Journeys in Faith: What happened to you and to your faith in the decades of the 1960s and 1970s? How do you see yourself, and the world, and the task of the Church as the decade of the 1980s unfolds?

It was an invitation to exercise that "flying fish" capacity we humans possess—to leap for a moment out of the stream of everydayness and, from that vantage point, look back to where we have been and ahead to what lies before us. Such looking, of course, is bound to be partial and as through a glass, darkly, as Paul reminds us, but nonetheless very much worth attempting. Thus like Abraham of old, I accepted the invitation and set out on a journey of remembering and anticipating, not knowing, as Abraham did not know, precisely where all this would end.

What happened to me and to my faith in the decades

of the 1960s and 1970s? In order to make some sense of the events in that period of my life, I need to reminisce even further—to set the stage, so to speak—about what I had brought with me to those particular years. I turned thirty in the Year of Our Lord 1960 and was well into "doing life" according to a pattern that stretched all the way back to my earliest beginnings.

How were those particular behavioral tracks laid down in the first place? I am not aware of any theory of early child development that can be trusted absolutely on this issue. Each person's functional life-style is a highly individualized combination of certain primitive perceptions of reality and the childhood vows that are made in response to those perceptions. At that stage of life, our powers of observation almost always exceed our powers of evaluation and interpretation. If this is not true of everyone, at least it was certainly true of me. I assimilated perceptually a great deal more than I understood properly, and in a very real sense, the significant changes that occurred in me religiously in the 1960s were corrections—the unlearning and the relearning—of certain perceptions and vows that I had embraced in the early 1930s.

What was my most primitive perception? The sense that I possessed no worth! Emptiness, a zero, a vacuum—these are the images that come to mind as I recall the way I felt about myself then. I have one clue to the source of that negative self-evaluation—I remember a statement that was often repeated by members of my family: If you are ever going to amount to anything, you must make something of yourself.

There is obviously a great deal of truth in this dictum, and I am sure the intention behind its repetition was basically a positive one. It was our family's way of motivating us children to actualize our potential, and they are not to be held accountable for my interpretation of its meaning. Each individual is finally responsible, I believe, for the consequences of an experience. We humans were given the power to "name the animals," according to the Genesis story. I take this to mean that we do not control the events that happen to us, but that we do determine the results of those events, their meaning in our lives. Thus the excessive blame-orientation that has so characterized recent times is misplaced, I feel. In evaluating my earliest reactions, I have concluded that I am the one who decided that the family dictum was descriptive rather than motivational. I am the one who chose to regard myself as a nobody, a nothing, a vacuum devoid of significance.

What was the childhood vow I made in response to my primitive perception? Not surprisingly, in light of where and when and what I happen to be, I vowed to become *homo competitus*, one who would acquire significance by outdoing others. Had I been born in another time or place or culture, the shape of my childhood vow might have been very different. But being American and middle class and white and male, it was fairly predictable that I would choose a life-style of competitiveness. This seemed the most obvious way for a nobody to become a somebody, for the terrible emptiness I perceived within to be filled with value and density.

And so, long before the decade of the 1960s, I

became a seasoned veteran in the game King of the Mountain and devoted much of my energy to getting ahead and achieving Willy Loman's dream of coming out Number One. I honestly believed that *achievement through strenuous effort* was the secret of life, and none of my experiences before the age of thirty-five managed to dislodge my perception of emptiness or my childhood vow to win by out-achieving everyone else.

This is not to say that all was serene or clear, once my approach to life was devised. Far from it! I can still recall the anxiety and fearfulness that were my constant psychic companions. There was hardly a time in my childhood or adolescence or young adulthood when I did not experience feelings of uncertainty and inadequacy when faced with certain challenges. Success depended upon my performance, and this only served to heighten my tension. It also served to isolate me from others in terms of real sharing and intimacy. I have always been a loner at heart, despite certain extroverted relational patterns I have worked to acquire, and I trace this fear-of-closeness tendency back to the old vow to compete. After all, how can one really establish authentic intimacy with those whom one is competing against and attempting to out-do? Inner anxiety, loneliness, drivenness—these were accompaniments to my chosen life-style, and none of the considerable religious experiences that were mine up until 1960 had much effect on my view of reality or on the way I "did" my life. Perhaps I should pause here to sketch those beginnings more fully.

I was raised in an intensely religious atmosphere. It

seemed that sacred language and symbols "came with my mother's milk," and participation in the institutional church was as much a part of my growing up as were meals at the family table. I have no memory of the moment when I first heard of God or Jesus or the realities of the Christian life, but somehow these beliefs did not connect creatively with my sense of self. How I could have heard from my birth that I was created by God, that God loved me so much that Jesus would die for me—how I could have heard that and still think that I had no worth, I cannot say. Again, all I can report is that those two realities never touched, although I continued to be active in church programs and, at the age of eighteen, decided to devote myself to the Christian ministry.

2 realities never touched

How was that decision made? I realize now that several strands of desire and need came together in my adolescent psyche to make such a vocation a reality. I had always been—and I remain until this day—deeply intrigued by the whole God-Reality and the dimension of the Transcendent. Long before I ever heard of Paul Tillich, I experienced a deep concern for the realm of the Ultimate, and one of the things that drew me positively to the ministry was the chance to work directly with this concern and grow in my understanding of it.

I also recall that an element of heroic idealism was a part of my call. Like many in my generation, I genuinely wanted to serve humanity and leave the world a better place for my having lived. Initially, I thought that becoming a medical doctor was the best means to this end, and I remember sharing this opinion with the physician who had cared for my family for many years. He was a gruff and direct sort of person, and when I said eulogistically, "You doctors help people so tangibly," he retorted, "Hell! What people need most is somebody to teach them how to live. I have lots of patients who get well and are still miserable." That chance remark was revolutionary in its impact on me. I thought, "Physical health is only a means to life—it is not the object of life. Teaching people how to live—that is the most tangible need." And as I looked about for ways to engage in that sort of task, the role of Christian minister seemed more to the point than any other.

But there was the push of my childhood vow as well. Even in the decision to become a minister, the realities of emptiness and achievement were at work. I believe that at least partially, my resolve to enter the ministry was an attempt to earn God's blessing. Given my perception of things, how else could that blessing be gained except by strenuous effort? I was also keenly aware of the acclaim and attention that older "church types" shower on a young person who "surrenders to the ministry," and I relished the prospect of such affirmation.

Most of all, however, I craved the approval of my mother—I longed to see a twinkle of delight in her eye and feel that she really was proud of me, something I had never felt before. There was always an atmosphere of marked anxiety in my mother's attitude toward my sister and me, especially when we were around members of her family. She seemed quite uneasy about how we were going to turn out. Being a seasoned manipulator by this time, I knew exactly what held the most promise of earning this particular reward. My grandfather had been a minister, and the church was the only institution that mattered to my mother. So in my calculating heart of hearts, I reasoned, "Becoming a minister will get my mother's approval," and this became a real factor in my decision. When I made my choice of career public and wrote my parents about it, I remember licking the envelope and saying with genuine anticipation, "Now, at last, I will be sparkled on by Mama!"

mother's approval

There was one other dynamic at work—the least noble of them all, yet one I should acknowledge, since it reflects my religious position at that time. To put the issue very bluntly: I decided to become a minister to improve my stature in campus politics. I was attending Mars Hill College in North Carolina. There was no student government—a religious organization known as the Baptist Student Union was the only campus-wide structure and thus represented the pinnacle of prestige. Remember, now, I was very much a nobody trying to become a somebody by out-achieving others. The presidency of the B.S.U. was a prize I very much wanted, and I was shrewd enough to realize that becoming a ministerial student would not hurt my candidacy for office. And so I acted.

campus politics

Events become much clearer upon reflection than when we actually lived them. I was hardly conscious of most of my motivations as I moved through childhood and adolescence, and I certainly would not have possessed the courage to admit them openly, had I been aware. Now, however, utilizing the discipline of meditation, I can perceive the real coherence that exists between my earliest perceptions and vows, and the subsequent developments. Human existence is not a jumble of isolated, unrelated particulars. What we decided long ago does affect the future. But this sense of coherence is not to be confused with fatalism or rigid determinism. Although we decide something at one point, we can redecide and redirect our energies at a later point, and that is what I began to attempt in the 1960s and 1970s. Such redirection never altogether eliminates the past. The old saying is true: I am where I am because I have been where I have been. But it helps us to understand and appreciate our pilgrimages more fully to remember the way we were—those primitive perceptions and subsequent childhood vows which unquestionably laid the tracks for developments to come.

2

Seeds Do Grow

The next steps in my life were fairly predictable. The various strands of motivation that influenced my decision to become a minister also represent the major components of my emerging personhood.

Behaviorally, I remained largely the product of my activistic culture and Protestant denomination. But my fascination with the realm of the Transcendent quickened and deepened during my college and seminary training, and I began to become dimly aware that some form of contemplation is the secret of wise activity. The Trappist monastery in Gethsemani, Kentucky, where Thomas Merton lived and worked, was only a short distance from the seminary in Louisville. We had a memorable experience in November of 1963—a visit to Gethsemani and an afternoon with Merton in his famous hermitage. I felt in that human being a kind of shalom—a warmth and openness that was deeply appealing. At the time, my

Merton

interest in contemplative disciplines was largely confined to reading about, rather than doing. However, a seed that would blossom eventually into something truly significant was slowly maturing.

I still retained that humanitarian idealism that wished to help humankind and leave this world a better place. I had always possessed an intuitive "feel" for other persons. Lewis Sherrill has suggested that very early in life, we make a fundamental choice between the human realm and the material realm—we decide which is of more value and holds the key to real fulfillment. Although I have no memory of making such a value-judgment, I believe that early on I opted for the human realm and thus developed a set of sensitivities for people. I was influenced also by the Christian emphasis on caring for one another. What happens to you makes a difference to me—this statement describes the ethos of my home and faith-community. By the early 1960s, I also had begun to feel a deep social and humanitarian concern. I had heard an Asian churchman pose a question that haunted me: "Why should any person on this earth have two coats until every person has one?" God knows, I have not lived out such radical egalitarianism literally, but neither have I ever been able to ignore such an ideal. Thus not surprisingly, a real concern for humanity, particularly those persons who are most oppressed, constituted another seed that continued to grow.

yes ↓
no —

Coupled with these dimensions, however, was the powerful momentum that I described previously—my drive to compete and to win, and thereby to acquire a sense of self-worth. This particular drivenness was never far away and continued to affect my actions and relationships. I had competed on all the fields of battle that make up the landscape of American college life—athletics, campus politics, social activity, and academic achievement—and had been relatively successful. However, after deciding on the vocation of ministry and entering seminary, I realistically tightened the focus of my concentration to academics. This proved to be an excellent move professionally, for I finished close to the top of my class. However, in terms of all-around personal development, I paid a real price for such one-sided accomplishment.

I made another crucial decision during that era—my marital decision—and it, also, was a result of my "deficiency motivation." I have alluded to the pressure to succeed that came from my family. My mother had been a schoolteacher, and it was important to her that her children excel academically. I remember her saying, "Bring me 100s and you'll see me smile." I valued my mother's approval so highly that I worked doubly hard to gain it, and this pattern must have carried over into the process of mate selection. Some say that we tend to marry people who have traits similar to those of our mothers or fathers, and looking back, I sense that this was true in my case. I felt that my mother had driven me relentlessly by remaining distant emotionally and offering approval only on the condition of success. And I picked a mate who related in precisely the same pattern. Somewhere deep inside I must have thought, "This is obviously the only kind of female who exists. She will push me as my mother did." Her hard-to-getness also activated my desire to prove myself by choosing and succeeding at the

choice of mate

toughest challenges I could find. The inherent flaws in
our relationship were a long time coming to final
flower, but they were present from the first and were
connected, at least in part, to my overwhelming desire
to earn a sense of well-being by accomplishment and
achievement.

The 1960s began with a highly significant event. In
the first year of the decade, I received what could be
called my big break professionally. Just before my
thirtieth birthday, I was called to be pastor of the
Crescent Hill Baptist Church in Louisville, Kentucky,
an institution of real prestige in our denomination,
with a congregation of some twenty-eight hundred
members. This tremendous leap up the ladder at that
stage of my career, in combination with the type of
person I was at that time, set the stage for an
eleven-year period of both anguish and growth.

I remember two things in particular about those
beginning days at Crescent Hill. First, I felt a
tremendous sense of elation—I had "arrived" professionally: I had obtained a job that gave me a significant
identity among my peers. During my seminary days, I
had wondered anxiously if I would ever have a chance
to make a name for myself. When I attended regional
and national conventions of our denomination, I had
felt so utterly anonymous. I would look with envy at
those in well-known positions and think, "If ever I
could get one of those jobs, my existence would have
density and substance. I would no longer be a kind of
plate-glass nonentity. If I held a prestigious post, all
would be different! People would look at me as if I
were *somebody*!" The position at Crescent Hill gave me
exactly the prestige I had craved.

But as always, more was involved than I had anticipated. I was like the prodigal son in Jesus' parable. In leaving home and going to the far country, he found precisely what he had wanted, but as he lived more deeply into the experience, he began to wonder if he really wanted what he had found. This was my reaction. It came as a real shock to discover the many responsibilities and heavy demands that accompany a position of prestige. I had simply wanted to *be* a person of renown. I had not realized that acclaim attends those positions because they are usually so hard to handle.

Years later, I heard the personnel manager of a national firm talk about the difference between people who simply want to *be* something and those who want to *do* something. The former type is dominated by an emptiness within. They are individuals who have not found a way to feed their ego needs healthily, and thus they attempt to use their jobs to enhance themselves. As a result, their judgment is usually clouded and their motives mixed. When faced with a significant decision, they always look at things on two levels. They ask, What ought to be done here for the sake of the company? But at a deeper level, they ask, What ought to be done here for *my* sake? How can I use this particular situation to advance my own cause? Such people can never risk or act courageously; they are, in fact, a liability to the company. "Part of my task," the personnel manager noted, "is to spot this type of personality as quickly as possible and weed those individuals out of significant decision-making posts."

The other type of people are those who want to *do* something. Their ego needs have been met healthily.

They have themselves off their hands, so to speak. These people look at a problem with a single purpose. They ask simply, What needs to be done here? What do the realities of the case require? They can make difficult decisions and act courageously. The personnel manager stated that one of his greatest challenges was to identify people of this stripe and move them up the hierarchy to decision-making positions as fast as possible.

When I heard this distinction later, light was shed on the paradoxical feelings that had been mine at the outset of my ministry at Crescent Hill. I realized then that I had been the type of individual who wanted to *be* something and that this accounted for my dismay and confusion over all the *doing* that went with a position of prestigious *being*!

But even in the early 1960s, it was quickly apparent to me that I had brought little inward agenda to this new opportunity. I had few deeply held convictions or unique gifts to share. My concerns were largely personal—I wanted others to regard me as an individual of worth. But lo and behold, what I had envisioned as the answer proved to be a cotton-candy experience. (I still remember how disappointed I was the first time I encountered that particular substance. To my six-year-old eyes, cotton candy had seemed the most heavenly delicacy imaginable. And so it proved to be—for a fleeting moment. I shall never forget that initial sensation of sweetness. But then—the emptiness, the tasting in one's mouth and finding only air!) That is the best analogy I know for the elation I experienced on beginning my first big job, only to discover that the excitement of *being* something evaporated quickly and left me face to face with a very different challenge: What do I *do* with the concrete opportunities open before me?

Since I had concluded long before that value was to be found outside, rather than inside my being, it is not surprising that at this juncture I turned to frenetic action. Why spend time exploring what the psalmist called "all that is within me," if I had decided ahead of time that emptiness was all that existed there? In deciding how to cope with this new challenge, I looked rather to voices outside myself.

Keith Miller once pointed out the functional importance of the question, Who is your audience? If what others think is a matter of crucial significance, then the identity of the particular set of individuals whose approval one prizes becomes crucial indeed. The values and thoughts of that group of "theys" will be formative in shaping one's behavior. On this point, *choose your audience* I have occasion to be very grateful, for the "audience" I picked turned out, on the whole, to be wise and mature in its Christian understanding, thus motivating me to do many right things, if not always for purely noble motives.

Parenthetically, let me pause to say that the realization that deeds are a mixture of good and evil is a potent source of hope in terms of God's grace and providence. In our fallen world, human activity is never purely good or purely evil. Some of our bad actions produce certain good effects serendipitously, and all our so-called good is a mixed reality at best.

So, largely motivated by others—several Crescent Hill members who had been in my old seminary community and who were now my chosen audience—I

began the task of "doing ministry." I wish that my
decision-making processes had been more genuinely
dialogical, that the inner realities had creatively
interacted with the outer realities to form wise choices.
Unfortunately, because of my sense of little inner
worth, my processes were almost totally monological—
what certain others thought about things proved
highly determinative. Yet I repeat—thanks be to God
for the kind of people those certain others were! They
believed that God was actively involved in the whole of
creation, seeking to redeem and complete it. They also
believed that Christians should join God, sacrificially
involving themselves in the same task. I believed this
vision to be utterly sound, and it tapped into much that
was healthy in me. So I plunged wholeheartedly into
the kind of activity that dominated American Protes-
tantism in the 1960s—vigorous social involvement. I
passionately wished the church to be relevant to the
day in which it lived; therefore the issues of racial
prejudice, poverty, and inhumane social structures
were foremost in my concern.

social activism

Needless to say, this understanding of the meaning
of the faith differed significantly from that of many
older lay people in the church. They were content to
sit on their comfortable pews within their stained-glass
ghettos and remain unconcerned about causes like
civil rights and poverty programs. Therefore my
emphasis on these causes created a great deal of
controversy.

My involvement with the issue of civil rights offers a
good illustration of these dynamics. I should mention
that I grew up in the South—Nashville, Tennessee, to
be exact—and I never realized there was a "race

problem" until I was a sophomore in college. My upbringing was a classic example of genteel prejudice. I was never exposed to the rabid racism that certainly flourished in many parts of the South, but I had always heard that the Negro should stay in his "place," meaning, of course, beneath our feet. To my subsequent chagrin, I recall that during my adolescence I joyfully joined my peers in yelling rude comments out of car windows at blacks.

It was not until the winter of 1949 that my awareness was genuinely altered. A truly outstanding Christian radical, Clarence Jordan of the Koinonia Farm in Georgia, came to speak at a Religious Emphasis Week at Mars Hill College, and in five short days, he literally turned my perceptual world upside down by applying biblical insight to the problem of racism. Jordan was trained at the same seminary I later attended, so the approach he took was reinforced during my years there, and it was also clearly supported by the audience in Crescent Hill whose approval I valued most. This fortified me for the conflicts that emerged during my ministry there.

I had become acquainted with Martin Luther King, Jr., while I was an assistant minister in Decatur, Georgia, and when he came to Louisville in 1961, I visited with him over a cup of coffee. Newspaper photographers happened to be nearby, and the next morning, my picture, seated at table with that highly controversial figure, appeared on the front page. Then all kinds of things began to happen. I began to receive angry phone calls and threatening letters. Sides began to form within the church family, for and against "the new preacher's modern ways."

Later that same year, a couple from Nigeria came to the seminary to study. They had written ahead, asking if they could join our church. They had no car, ours was the only church within walking distance, and they were direct products of our missionary activity. I saw this as a clear-cut area of Christian responsibility, although no black person had ever been welcomed to worship with us, much less permitted to join the church.

When I consulted our deacon board, I quickly learned which issues had priority in situations like this. Most of the people there had backgrounds similar to my own—they were not rabid racists, but simply had gone along with the southern way of life. Thus they themselves were not strongly opposed to the idea of African members, but they feared that such an action at that time would disrupt the church. "We will lose members and money," they predicted, "and we will become known as a radical church." Concern for the institution was greater than concern for the issue. I rose to the occasion that night. I argued persuasively, I believe, that compromise on an issue of this magnitude would do more to destroy the institution's future than would costly integrity. I remember urging, "We are not called by Christ to be successful, but faithful." For a person who valued success as much as I did, that represented real growth.

I am happy to report that after much discussion, the majority of those present voted to recommend that the couple be received. A few Sundays later, this was done—amid much murmuring, but done, nonetheless.

We did lose a number of members and some money, as had been predicted, but we also gained other members because of our stand, and as a congregation, we began to move more clearly in a progressive direction.

As for myself, I became irrevocably imaged as a liberal and a controversialist. I found I had a variety of feelings about that image. I was somewhat frightened by the open hostility and threats that came my way. I did not enjoy the anonymous letters that poured in for years. I was troubled by the abuse that occasionally befell my wife and children. However, through it all, the audience I had chosen stayed solidly with me; that support reinforced my humanitarian leanings and empowered me to cope with opposition. So I continued to plot a course of active social involvement.

The issue of race was my dominant, but by no means exclusive concern at that time. My old question—Why should anyone have two coats until everyone has one?—made me very sensitive to the poverty programs that developed in that era. I was convinced that economic issues were foundational to all others, and I was anxious to be part of the answer and not part of the problem. I served on a variety of boards during those days and even considered leaving the ministry to become the executive of a government agency. I decided not to do so out of a rather clear sense of my own personal gifts. It had become obvious that I had the ability to enlighten and inspire people through the pulpit and other word-event occasions. I was an adequate, but not highly effective administrator and organizer. As I pondered the actual work I would be doing, I felt strongly that the opportunities open to me as one of the concerned clergy were better suited to my gifts. I have never regretted that choice.

The ecumenical foment among Protestants and Catholics in the 1960s also drew my attention. I had never been comfortable with the attitude of my particular denomination in relation to other parts of the Body of Christ. Southern Baptists had remained aloof from the conciliar ecumenical movements of the 1940s and 1950s. That stance, in part, was a result of the arrogant notion that we alone had the truth and should not mix with those in error. It was tied also to the suspicion and fear that had originated after the Civil War when the defeated South was disparaged by other national groups. I for one felt it was time that Southern Baptists came out of their isolation, to both give to and receive from other groups. Thus I became the "token Southern Baptist" in innumerable local and national ecumenical endeavors. Again, the seminary had cultivated this broader sensitivity, and by and large, my audience at Crescent Hill was with me.

My position on our nation's involvement in South Vietnam received less unified support. The gradual development of my thought on this matter was not particularly unusual. At first I was uneasy, but had no deep convictions about the actions of President Johnson. However, as our involvement deepened and the real nature of that conflict appeared to be a civil war that concerned largely Vietnamese, I began to voice my sentiments more openly.

When I was selected to preach the annual sermon at the Southern Baptist Convention in 1971, I decided to address this issue. I used the parable of the prodigal son as my text, designating the United States as the prodigal and Vietnam as our "far country." We had gone there, like the younger son, out of a mixture of

arrogance, idealism, and naïveté, and there we had
been forced "to come to ourselves" in terms of our real
limits. But I offered hope—if the church could act
toward our nation as the wise loving father had acted
toward the prodigal, we could learn from our pain and
assume a constructive role among the family of
nations.

The sermon provoked strong reactions. Many
individualistic pietists resented the discussion of a
political issue in a religious gathering. Several right-
wing conservatives were incensed that I would
compare America to the "sinful" prodigal. In the
uproar that ensued, I became more convinced than
ever of John Gardner's observation that America was
caught in the brutal crossfire between "unloving critics
and uncritical lovers." I intended to be neither, but "a
discerning, honest lover of my country."

Looking back, I am pleased both with the note I
struck and that I chose to strike that note. I believe that
what I said then has stood the test of time, that it
represented an early awareness which the general
public came to feel later. I know there are many
definitions for the ability of a prophet, but this is one I
favor: A prophet can penetrate deeply enough into
present reality to see in which direction the currents
are flowing. I believe that at that time, I participated in
a prophetic effort.

I have mentioned my decision to stay in the clergy
role because of the opportunities it provided on the
conceptual level. I tried to make the most of that
particular activity and during the 1960s, developed a
fairly good balance between study, reflection, and
spoken and written output. It was never easy, but I was

aided by my perfectionistic tendencies and usually devoted about twenty to thirty hours a week to study and preparation.

Looking back, then, I would say that for the most part, I am pleased with the extent of my participation in the many issues of the 1960s. I believe I was right more times than wrong. However, to be fully honest, I recall some things with regret. First, my motivation was often highly mixed at best. Acquisition was still a dominant concern and I often wonder what would have happened had I picked a different audience, or had they turned against me. I had relatively little inner agenda and so great a need to gain the approval of others that I honestly do not know what I would have done if I had been called upon to walk that lonesome valley alone. I think I know, and this makes me slow to criticize and full of compassion for those who crumple under pressure—those who, in order to get along, go along.

That inner emptiness also clouded my judgment and sometimes involved me in certain projects which my own sensitivities told me were unwise, but which I did not have the courage to oppose. A case in point was the Poor People's March on Washington sponsored by The Southern Christian Leadership Conference after Dr. King's death. I was the treasurer of the Kentucky affiliate of that organization, since its leaders had become another audience whose approval I very much wanted. I was so afraid of being accused of not being committed to the movement that I failed to say what I honestly thought about certain issues. The group was thus deprived of some perhaps unwelcome but reality-based insight.

I believe many white liberals shared the same experiences during those days. In reaction to the position that depicted blacks as all-bad, we went to the other extreme, viewing victims of oppression as all-good. I subsequently came to affirm what Kyle Haseldon said so movingly: "Our equality does not lie in the fact that we are as good as each other as much as in the fact that we are as bad as each other and in equal need of redemption." Haseldon's goal of giving to each black what we would give to any human being, and expecting of each black what we would expect of any human being is the authentic ideal, but my actions in the past fell short of that goal. My need to *be* something was still so great that it affected the patterns of my doing and discerning. For all the good feelings I have about much that was accomplished, there is a certain sadness as well.

3

Shadows at Noonday

Somewhere in the middle of the 1960s, several things began to stir in my subterranean depths that even I in my compulsiveness could not ignore. The term *mid-life crisis* is now a household commonplace, thanks to Gail Sheehy, Daniel Levinson, innumerable other authors, and talk shows. When I first began to experience mine, I did not know what to call it, but that did not lessen its intensity or unsettling quality. And although it would have removed some of the shame and fearfulness to realize that my problem was part of a larger pattern all humans undergo, the challenge of coping with it would have remained. Knowing that thousands of other people also experience toothache does not eliminate one's struggle with a very real and localized pain.

Several factors contributed to my new experience of unease. Part of the trouble was purely physical. For years, I had been driving myself at a relentless pace. I had made it a habit to get up at five o'clock every morning to ensure some study time before the hectic demands of the day. I took no regular day off, nor did I have a specific exercise program. I had always been able to reach back for that extra energy to meet every new demand, but suddenly one day that pattern failed—when I reached back, I found nothing there but total exhaustion. At about that same time, I had my first experience with sexual impotence. Then signs of high blood pressure showed up during a routine physical examination. In my middle thirties, I was having my first existential taste of the limits inherent in human existence.

Robert Raines has pointed out that in *Fiddler on the Roof,* it is on the occasion of his daughter's wedding—a classic mid-life episode—that Teyve begins to sing of "sunrise, sunset," suddenly realizing that there is a terminus point of life, as well as a beginning point. When one is young, it seems that one can go on forever. The fact of death is recognized intellectually, but not emotionally. But when energy begins to fail and, for the male particularly, when sexual vitality begins to show signs of diminishing, it occurs to one that life *does not go on forever.* The impact of this realization is awesome indeed. This experience of peaking out physically and starting the gentle decline has been described as the first inkling of incipient death.

But of course, I was undergoing far more than bodily changes. I was also feeling the pressures that were the inevitable outcome of the way I had invested my energies in earlier years. Gail Sheehy has listed three basic components that make up a human being:

Sheehy

the vocational—one's creative achievement; the relational—one's interaction with significant others; and the realm of inwardness—the part of oneself that is genuinely unique and is expressed simply for one's own private delight. Sheehy suggests that all of us tend to overinvest in one or the other of these components in our earlier years and that during the mid-adult crisis, the effects of this imbalance begin to surface. Then we are forced to reassess the way we are spending our energies, and we must make whatever adjustments are called for. The most common symptom at such a time of upheaval is the lessening of satisfaction in those areas where one has invested too much, together with an upsurge of interest in the areas previously neglected. Sheehy also points out that, particularly in white middle-class America, men and women tend to experience this crisis of life very differently.

male sequence

In his twenties and thirties, the average American male, as my story so richly corroborates, usually overinvests in the vocational side of life. He may have many relationships up to the mid-life point, Sheehy claims, but only one real love affair, and that is with his job or career. "Making it" professionally is the goal impressed on the male psyche from the moment of birth. As a rule, the realms of inwardness and relationships come in a distant second in the allocation of energies. How, then, does mid-life reassessment manifest itself? Suddenly, the pull of work begins to lessen; the need for more intimate relationships and more opportunity to pursue private enthusiasms pushes to the surface. The male may either find that he has fulfilled all the goals he set for himself professionally, or realize that he never will be able to reach them and must renegotiate with his dreams. But in neither case are such concerns quite as all-consuming as the vocational realm once was. Where are the people with whom I can share the journey of life? How can I find time to do the things that bring me joy? These become his new concerns, setting the stage for a whole new direction of development.

While this is going on in the average male, a very different phenomenon may be occurring in the female, for her early conditioning was very different. She has tended to overinvest her early years in the relational side of life, helping her husband in his career and caring for and nurturing children. The mid-life realignment of the white middle-class American female tends to move in the direction of the vocational, or achieving, realm. A woman of thirty-five or forty begins to think about entering or re-entering the marketplace, so either going back to school or finding a job becomes a main concern.

From these observations, it is not hard to see why the divorce rate among couples in their late thirties and early forties is so high. If the husband and wife are not aware of what is happening within themselves, no wonder there is a head-on collision on the road both are traveling! At the very moment the workaholic male begins to reach out to relate more deeply to his wife, she suddenly is nowhere to be found. She is busily engaged in the very area of which her husband has begun to tire. Such "crossing over" can be handled creatively and can make for even better marriages, but only if both mates clearly recognize what is happening and each grants the other flexibility in moving on to the next stage.

When these insights came to me later, they helped to illumine my concerns of the mid-1960s. At that time the very things I have just described began to surface very noticeably. The compulsion to succeed was beginning to relax its hold a bit. Was this because of disappointment? Possibly. I was now experiencing fully many of the things I had earlier thought would bring satisfaction. The analogy of cotton candy again came to mind. In my seminary days I had said to myself, "If only I could be called to a prestigious pulpit . . . be asked to speak at a Southern Baptist Convention . . . appear on the program at our national assembly grounds . . . be elected to some denominational office—then I would *be* somebody and at last taste the density of significance within." But now all those things were happening, and they were by no means as satisfying as I had anticipated.

Then, too, how much is ever *enough* on the treadmill of success? Not only was I disappointed by the actual taste of achievement, but I found the whole business so elusive. No sooner did I manage to reach one pinnacle than two other higher and more difficult peaks appeared. If I preached a really fine sermon, the reaction of the crowd was "More! More! Let's see if you can top this one." For the first time in my life, I began to question seriously the primitive perceptions and childhood vows that had shaped my life. Was fame, reknown, the approval of others—in a word, success— really as valuable as I had thought? Or was William James indeed accurate years ago when he labeled it a bitch-goddess?

Coupled with the waning of the desire for success was a growing sense of loneliness as a person, a certain hollowness at the center of my being. I had many, many contacts in those days—my congregation was large and my network of professional connections extensive—but I had very few deep relationships. There were several reasons for this. Lack of time was one. I was so busy studying and doing well and achieving that I simply had created no structure on which profound friendships could grow. Competition and manipulation were other contributing factors. When one is forever trying to get ahead and out-do other people, it is difficult to experience deep mutuality with them. But most of all, I suppose, that pervasive sense of having no worth within kept me from opening up deeply to others. I did not want others to see into my depths, for I was genuinely ashamed of the lack I felt there. Yet the Book is right: It is not good for humankind to be alone. For the first time, I hungered for I/thou forms of sharing, to be with another in delight and ease, to take part in one of the great graces of life.

Undoubtedly, that sense of aloneness was intensified by the lack of intimate sharing in our home life. All the factors I have just identified played a part in creating that situation—lack of time, overinvestment in career, deep uneasiness about allowing my depths to be really known by others. Added to these, however, was my lack of courage to face openly the relational lacks I was experiencing. Neither my wife nor I had grown up in homes of vibrant intimacy, so we were both genuine amateurs there. Although from the very beginning I had not been satisfied with the level of our mutuality—our sharing of values, experiences, feelings, knowledge, sexuality—when I had mentioned this, my wife had responded fearfully and defensively and had withdrawn even more.

This pattern frustrated me deeply, yet the risk of further confrontation seemed too great. The contemporary minister is in a double bind, since one's failure at marriage usually means the loss of one's profession. As a result, I drew back and developed a very perfunctory, matter-of-fact arrangement at home, giving up all hope of authentic intimacy. In retrospect, that failure of nerve on my part was a costly mistake. At that early stage of our marriage, neither my wife nor I acted as we should have in order to meet our primal relational needs healthily. My compulsion to succeed had overridden the need for intimacy, but such a value-judgment could not sustain itself forever and contributed mightily to the loneliness that continued to assert itself as I grew older and more and more disconnected.

There was also the problem of the hollowness at the center of my being. Up to that point, I had no hobbies or avocations to speak of. Work and family constituted the two poles of my functional existence. Once I asked an acquaintance, a seminary professor, why he invested such considerable time and energy in raising both flowers and vegetables. He answered simply, "For my own satisfaction. I do not do it to make money or to impress anyone. It is an enthusiasm that is part of my individual uniqueness, and I give expression to it for private delight alone." At earlier stages in my life, I had regarded such an expenditure of energy as a waste of precious time, but as the winds of change blew through my being, I found myself strangely wistful and even envious of that man. There was nothing in my existence comparable to gardening. Frankly, the idea that perhaps I had latent possibilities that could and should be nurtured had never occurred to me. And why should it? Given my old reality-conclusion, I was an emptiness, a void, a vacuum that must be filled from the outside, if there were to be worth within.

It should be obvious that my mid-adult crisis was much the same as that of most human beings—unsettling and disconcerting. In the most literal sense, old things were passing away and all things were being made new. Such transitions are rarely simple or easy. The prospect of change almost always evokes ambiguous inner feelings, for by its very nature, change involves giving up some of what we have and receiving other things we did not heretofore possess. This loss/gain polarity is inherent in any experience worthy of the name *change,* but usually our human tendency is to focus more on what we must relinquish than on what we are about to receive. Thus at the time, I was more alarmed than excited. I recall being profoundly uneasy about what it all meant and where it was going to lead.

4

Experiencing Grace

In the midst of my mid-life crisis, something happened that proved to be positively electrifying in altering my consciousness of reality itself. The greatest single shift in my whole existence—from seeing life in terms of acquisition to seeing it in terms of awareness—took place in 1965, in an unforgettable way.

I received a call late one Monday afternoon from a Presbyterian friend, one of the leading ministerial lights of our city. He was an excellent preacher, a dynamic community leader, and had been the prime mover in developing one of the fastest growing suburban congregations in Louisville.

But that afternoon there was a note of exhaustion and desperation in his voice. He came right to the point:

Listen, John. I am in real trouble personally. Where does a pastor go for pastoral care? We are so busy ministering to everybody else that we never have an opportunity to find help for our own needs.

So I decided this afternoon to call five of you whom I trust. Would you be willing to meet once a week for two months, to see if we can form some structure of ministry? The only agenda would be honesty and openness and an attempt to do what we can for each other. I don't know if this will help, but if it doesn't, I'm afraid I'm about to go under.

My reaction was complete shock! I was so startled by this cry for help that I could hardly answer. For one thing, I could not believe that someone who appeared so competent outwardly could be encountering the kind of problems he described. But even more unbelievable was his willingness to acknowledge his need and reach out for help. Such an action flies straight in the face of the conditioning of American males from day one. Be a little man . . . Mother's little soldier . . . don't cry or show emotion . . . learn to bear pain . . . keep a stiff upper lip—these are the messages ground into our gender from birth.

Carlyle Marney once observed that the average American male probably needs pastoral care more from age thirty-five to forty-five than at any other time in his life and *is least likely to get it*, for the simple reason that he is ashamed to admit weakness or the need for outside assistance. I was as astonished by my friend's courage as by his need, and his call set in motion a flood of conflicting emotions.

How should I respond to this cry for help and the proposed solution? The professional minister in me was moved to reach out caringly, as I would to any person in distress—I, the strong one, compassionately stooping to help the weak. But this situation was more complicated. All the feelings of my mid-adult transition were very close to the surface, and the desperation in my colleague's voice activated my own fears and anxieties. I remember thinking, "Will I be able to maintain the posture of a rescuer in this situation? Who knows—this man's honest expression of his problems might trigger in me a corresponding confession."

Quite frankly, I cringed at the thought of acknowledging my present emotional state to the other clergy he was proposing to call. They were men with whom I was cordial at the professional level, but in a deeper sense, they were the very ones with whom I felt most competitive. "One wants to appear only at one's best in front of people like that," I thought to myself, and on the strength of that alone, I almost claimed a schedule conflict so that I could bow out of the whole process.

And yet . . . if one is hurting badly enough, one is moved to risk almost anything. All the confusion and loneliness and hollowness of which I was becoming increasingly aware cried out to oppose my fear. I almost said to my friend, "Do you think you are the only one who is about to go under? If you only knew the load that is about to sink my boat." And deep within me, something whispered, "Maybe this is what you have been looking for all along. After all, there has to be some better way than this everlasting drive to acquire worth by competition. Perhaps a band of brothers could help." So, hesitant and fearful, I told my friend that I would come the next morning and participate in his experiment.

I slept very little that night. Apprehension over this new venture of openness and what I might be getting into kept my mind racing.

Interestingly enough, every minister who had been approached on such short notice the day before showed up—a significant fact in itself! That Tuesday morning marked the beginning of the most important transition I had ever known.

I should mention that all this occurred before the small-group movement came into such prominence in the life of the church. Thus it was a new form of experience to me. I received my seminary training in the 1950s, when academic interaction was the sole form of learning. The "clinical pastoral education" emphasis, which helps ministers experientially internalize the great concepts of Christianity, had not come into its own at that time. "Between my ears," I knew all about grace, and justification by faith, and mercy, and forgiveness, but, to quote the great black preacher Howard Thurman, "the other parts of me had not yet heard the Word." Grace was a *concept* to me at that time—not an event in which I participated to the depths of my being. That momentous shift was about to occur.

the "other parts"

I watched and listened with some uneasiness as the masks started to come off and the first wounds and needs were identified. The process was begun by the man whose cry for help had called us together, but before long we all were involved. I remember being utterly astonished by two things during the first session. It was amazing how much alike the six of us were, even though we came from a wide range of religious and social backgrounds. When one lives as isolated from the depths of others as our competitive way of life demanded, one concludes that the shadows within oneself are abnormal—that no one else experiences such darkness. But as the veils were pulled aside, I was astounded to find that we all felt similar conflicts and pressures. Miguel Unamuno once said: "If we would ever get honest enough to go out in the streets and uncover our common griefs, what we would discover is that we are all grieving for the self-same things." How true those words are in terms of the discoveries that emerged around our little circle!

My other surprise was that honesty evoked compassion. One assumption central to my competitive mind-set was that weakness would be exploited if ever revealed. I had always tried to put my best foot forward and hide the rest as much as possible. But an opposite law was at work in that setting. I am not naïve enough to think that all small sharing groups could be similarly mature and redemptive, but in our group of six, it never failed: When one of us dropped his facade and shared the way he really felt—rather than being ridiculed or abused, he was invariably surrounded by understanding and concern and insight. Paul's words—"There is therefore now no condemnation" (Rom. 8:1)—literally characterized the interaction between us in that pastor's study.

It was all so new and intriguing and relevant to my need that I soon did what I had suspected I might do, when the idea had been initially proposed. I took off my mask—for the first time in my life—and went all the way back and all the way down to those earliest reality-conclusions that had shaped my life so power-fully. I acknowledged the bottomless feeling of nobodiness, the desperate need to acquire a sense of worth by my own strenuous effort, the never-ending desire to become famous and *be somebody* in the eyes of others. Event after event was recalled and revealed. It was as if I had lanced a boil and all the infected pus was gushing forth. Not even I had realized how much pain and agony were accumulating in my depths over those decades. But it all came out that morning, in what was a frightening and yet a cleansing experience.

When I was finished—literally spent, like one who has vomited out the last undigested particle—something happened that I shall never forget. The man in the group for whom I felt the least natural affinity was the first to speak. He was an Episcopal priest, socially prominent and much more liberal theologically than I. Of all those present, he was the last I would have expected to speak the Word of God to my depths. But so it was, in the providence of the God whose other name is always Surprise, that he began, "I hear you, John, oh, I hear you! I've walked that same road, felt those same things." Then he went on:

Do you know what we need? [I noticed that he did not use the isolating, condemning "what *you* need," but the inclusive *we*.] We need to hear the gospel down in our guts. Do you remember in the Sermon on the Mount, when Jesus said "You are the light of the world"? He did not say that you have to earn light or become number one in order to get light. He said simply, "You *are* light." If you and I could ever hear that down in our guts—really experience what it means, then we could do what Jesus goes on to say:

We could let our light shine, and other people could see the good thing God has created and give glory to the Father in heaven.

As he spoke those words, I felt something akin to fire flow from the top of my head to the depths of my heart, and for the first time in my life I *experienced* grace—it was not thought about or understood conceptually, but happened to me in the way events do sometimes happen to one. It was like being drenched to the skin by a rain shower and knowing that it has made one genuinely and vastly different.

There are many images I could use to describe the miraculous thing that happened to me that day, but the title of this book is the best, I think—*my eyes were opened* in that instant as never before. I began to "see" myself and eventually all things in a completely different light. It suddenly dawned on me that I had been mistaken all along in my conclusions about reality. Instead of being an emptiness that must be filled from without by strenuous effort, I was, in fact, a fullness by the creative act of God. There had been worth in me from the very beginning—not by virtue of what I had made of myself, but by virtue of what God had made of me in calling me out of nothingness into being. The words of Paul suddenly took on new significance: "By the grace of God *I am what I am*" (I Cor. 15:10).

In that moment my perceptual world was literally turned upside down, and the movement from acquisition to awareness began. All my life, I had thought that in order to have worth, it is necessary to bring what is outside in, but at that moment, I saw that it is the other way around: The challenge is to become aware of what is already inside by the grace of creation and to learn to bring that fullness out through generous and sacrificial service to the whole creation.

Some time after that, I heard Sam Keen describe a similar episode in his pilgrimage, and certain images he used helped to illuminate my own. He had begun his journey, as I had, with a sense of nobodiness and a need for density and significance. He chose the way of academic achievement as a means of acquiring worth, thinking, "If I could only be accepted into an Ivy League college . . . go to graduate school . . . earn a doctorate . . . become a professor . . ."—and he had traveled that road for twenty-five years. As each of those milestones was reached, the old cotton-candy sensation had recurred—a moment of intense satisfaction and then the sense of emptiness again.

After Keen became a professor, he had achieved yet another of his goals by reading a paper before a learned society. Afterward, he found himself alone and desperate in a hotel room. Then that sophisticated, secular man got down on his knees and cried out, "What must I do to be saved? . . . What on earth must I do?" And suddenly on the wall before him appeared these words: "Nothing! Nothing at all! It comes with the territory or it does not come at all!" At that moment, an old Zen image came to his mind—a man "riding on an ox, looking for an ox"—and Keen realized that it could represent himself.

What a graphic image—riding on an ox while looking for an ox! That described me as well! For thirty-five years I had been searching, straining, looking everywhere outside myself for the worth I needed! And that morning in the study of a Presbyterian minister, I saw for the first time that the "ox" had been beneath me—that the worth had been within me all along—yet I had never perceived it!

I did not in that moment become an utterly different creature—the change was in *my awareness of myself*. What the encounter on the Damascus Road was to Saul of Tarsus, the tower episode to Martin Luther, and the Aldersgate incident to John Wesley, those words, "You *are* the light of the world," were to me. That experience opened up a whole new beginning for me—a whole new way to see myself and reality as a whole, and I cannot overstate its transforming impact.

Yet I want to underline the word *beginning*. The weakness of so much conversionist terminology is that it seems to deny the process-nature of human experience. When one exclaims, "Once I was blind, but now I see," it can easily be construed to mean that everything is instantly and totally altered and that the new bears no resemblance to the old. In attempting to do justice to the genuineness of a change-experience, it is easy to overstate the case. I do not want to do that. I readily acknowledge that God had been very much at work during all those years leading up to that moment of new insight. Just as vigorously, I affirm that learning to live with that altered awareness has been a gradual, inch-by-inch process. Some seventeen years after that life-giving moment, I am still in the process of internalizing it more fully and of rooting that vision more deeply in the whole of my being. We set people up for disillusionment, I believe, when we claim too total a transformation for any one experience. "First the seed, then the blade, then the flower"—that seems to be God's way of doing things.

Elizabeth O'Connor claims that the famous Great Commission in Matthew 28 has an internal, as well as an external meaning. Jesus said, "Go ye therefore, and teach all nations, baptizing them in the name of the Father, and of the Son, and of the Holy Ghost." O'Connor thinks that this can refer to "our many selves within" as well as to peoples of other lands and cultures. I affirm this insight wholeheartedly. I can think of no better description of these last years than that they have been spent in an attempt to appropriate more fully "the length and depth and height and width" of the new awareness of reality that came to me that day.

The process of assimilation has been not only gradual, but uneven and erratic, much more like riding a roller coaster than an escalator. I identify deeply with the story of a medieval peasant woman who happened to meet a Benedictine monk. She fell down before him and blurted out, "Please tell me, holy father, what do you men of God do up there in the monastery on the hill? It appears to be so close to heaven. How do you spend your days and hours?" That particular monk was wise and humble, and he answered simply, "What do we men of God do up there in the monastery so close to heaven? I will tell you, my child: We fall down and we get up! We fall down and we get up! We fall down and we get up!" How typical this is of all human growth!

Something truly revolutionary happened to me that day, but one does not put off the old and put on the new the way one changes coats. In the days that followed my new awareness, I often found myself falling back into old habits, feeling again the "nobodiness" that drove me to compete.

I can sympathize both with those new Christians in Galatia and with Paul's frustration at their slow rate of growth. Before hearing the good news, they, too, had thought that worth was something to be earned. Products of first-century Judaism, they had attempted to earn worth by keeping the Law: They were circumcised, followed dietary restrictions, and obeyed all the other rules. Then Paul came and told them his story—that he, too, had striven to earn God's righteousness by perfect obedience, only to discover that he could not—and, more important, that in Jesus Christ *he did not need to!* Worth is a gift, not a reward, Saul had discovered. We humans do not need to earn our way into the Kingdom; we will *inherit* it, by virtue of the One to whom we are related—we are sons and daughters of God!

All this Paul had shared, and the Jews in Galatia had received it. The apostle had been used by God to facilitate that most important of redemptive tasks—opening the eyes of the blind—and the Galatians had begun to see and taste the glorious gift that God has given all humans through Jesus Christ.

But when Paul left the region, certain representatives of the old ways (Judaizers, they were called) attempted to reestablish the former patterns. Word came to Paul that those who had tasted of the freedom of grace had fallen back into the old ways of earning. His Epistle deals with this very issue. "How could you?" he asks.

But of course, at least part of the answer lies in our nature as human beings. We grow and change only gradually. That was certainly true of my experience. Like Abraham of old, I had been touched by a new vision of reality and had set out on a radically different way. But there are "many miles and lots of steps" before I reach the Promised Land.

5

Learning to
Do Differently

Several milestones in that process of growing in grace are worth noting. In the spring of 1967, I spent six weeks on a fellowship in continuing education at the Virginia Seminary, just outside Washington, D.C. An ecumenical venture including seven clergy, and centering on the overall theme of understanding and coping with change as it is experienced personally, societally, and ecclesiastically, this proved to be an intensification of the sort of group encounter I had first tasted two years before. It served to challenge me, particularly in applying my new realization to the area of work and vocation.

The months immediately after I had discovered the "ox" beneath me had been focused primarily on self-exploration. "So there is something of value within me after all," I had exclaimed, and with new curiosity, I had taken up a search for the treasure that had been placed there by my Creator. I began to uncover gifts and potentials and interests that were a surprise even to me, and a spirit of adventure, rather than the fiends of drivenness, began to stir gently within.

My attitude toward my work also had begun to undergo alteration, although it was not until the study episode in Virginia that I squarely faced that sector of my life and began to deal with those traits that are always hardest to change—behavioral patterns. As I have noted, I had been working seven days a week and doing almost nothing else, with the exception of family activities. Even before the coming of grace, I had seen clearly that this way of life was not tenable, but during my sabbatical I realized that it was as *unnecessary* as it was *unwise*. Since I had discovered that there was worth within, I did not *need* to work so desperately to find density or to fill up emptiness!

Then, too, the opinion of others was gradually losing some of its tenacious hold. Years before, I had learned that public opinion could be a fickle goddess. Duffy Dougherty, on retiring as head football coach at Michigan State University, said that the trouble with his profession was that one is "responsible to irresponsible people." This applies as well to others' opinions of one. Sometimes one receives far more than deserved in terms of praise or criticism, and sometimes far less, depending on the maturity of one's chosen audience. I began to realize that work is far more authentic as a process for giving gifts than for earning applause. There was a shift, then, in my consciousness, toward becoming more aware of that which God had placed within me and in considering how this could be appropriately shared with others.

The old feverish concern, What do others want of me and how can I possibly gain their approval? began to diminish.

It is never easy to break out of old routines and develop new ones, but the six weeks' retreat in Virginia helped to generate new motivation for doing just that. I went back to work armed with the resolve to cut down on quantity and to be more inwardly directed. What *I* felt and thought and needed would, for the first time, at least receive a hearing. Slowly I learned to say no without feeling guilty. I began to take a whole day off, as well as play handball once or twice a week. Most significant, perhaps, I started to stand up to some of my black friends who occasionally asked me to things I deemed unwise. I do not yet feel fully redeemed in the area of work, for the pressures within are still strong, but the new tracks that were laid down in 1967 have vastly affected my physical and emotional well-being, and also the quality of my creativity.

Another large milestone in my growth in grace was passed when I was initiated into the great fraternity of the bereaved as the decade of the 1970s began. My wife and I had two beautiful children—a son and namesake born in 1958, and a daughter, Laura Lue, in 1959. Although very different in makeup and temperament, they both were sheer delights. Then came the crushing blow in July of 1968—Laura Lue was suffering from acute leukemia. I have chronicled the story of her illness and subsequent death, and my reactions to it, in the little book *Tracks of a Fellow Struggler,* and I shall not repeat those here. However, no account of my faith-journey would be complete

without reference to that experience and to the way it
fits into the movement from acquisition to awareness.

What I saw about myself and all reality so vividly in
1965 undergirded me when I was called upon to
relinquish a relationship with one I loved very deeply.
That day in the study of my friend, the truth came
home to me that life is gift. If I am not a void that must
be filled by strenuous effort . . . if I have already been
created . . . if I am the light of the world by virtue of
God's action . . . then of course that is true of all others
as well, including dear Laura Lue. Learning to apply
that vision to her life and death was one of the greatest
challenges I have yet faced.

I was enormously helped by Gerhard von Rad's
interpretation of the biblical episode in which Abraham was told to offer his son Isaac as a sacrifice. That
whole chapter—Genesis 22—had always presented
real difficulties for me. But von Rad, in *Genesis, A
Commentary*, claims that Yahweh's purpose was to
discover whether Abraham remembered how the
religion of promise had originated, and how it was
intended to function. From the beginning, events had
been controlled by Yahweh, not by Abraham—they
resulted from Yahweh's grace and gift, not from
Abraham's earning or acquiring. And what was true of
all things was true, of course, of Isaac, the long-
awaited heir who seemed to be Abraham's sole link
with the future. How easy it would have been for
Abraham to cherish Isaac more than he loved
Yahweh, or to regard Isaac as his very own possession.
Earlier in his faith-journey, Abraham had attempted
to take things into his own hands, to create his own
security, and von Rad believes that Yahweh used this

method to see whether Abraham had in fact matured.
Did he remember where Isaac had come from, to
whom he really belonged, and that all things—even
this beloved son—were gifts, not wages or rewards?
On Mount Moriah, our father in faith made it clear
that he had matured and that he did remember. I
found von Rad's perspective vastly helpful in those
days after my beloved one had suffered and died.

One's great temptation in moments of bereavement
is to give way to resentment or despair. One can easily
blow up in anger or sink down in hopelessness,
honestly feeling that there is simply nothing left to live
for—no future, really, only a bleak landscape of
emptiness. In the days immediately following Laura
Lue's death, I was no stranger to either of these
feelings. "What kind of God are you?" I sometimes
raged. "Why would you allow an innocent little girl to
suffer as she did and then die? What right did you
have to take away the one I cherished?" At other
moments I felt no anger at all; in fact, that was the
problem: *I felt nothing at all.* It was as if most of me had
died, too. I could not see anything in the Great Not Yet
that appeared important enough to justify getting up
in the morning.

If I had not had at least a taste of reality as grace, I
honestly do not know how I could have made it
through the valley of the shadow of death. There was
nothing in my old vision of emptiness and effort and
earning that could have confronted the emotions that
loomed on all sides. However, the awareness that all is
given—that value exists not because of what we have
done, but because of what God has done—gave me a
different outlook on both the past and the future.

Who was Laura Lue, really? She had been a gift—not something I had created and therefore had the right to clutch as an owned possession, but a treasure who had always belonged to Another. She had been with me solely through the gracious generosity of that One. Had Laura Lue been my *God would have been a thief* possession by right, then God would, in fact, have been a thief, and anger on my part would have been justified. But on the premise that nothing actually belongs to us—that all is given—anger seemed inappropriate. The vision that first broke over me in relation to my own being thus extended to include Laura Lue and that, more than anything else, kept me from the rage and resentment that so often follow an experience of grief and can become a corrosive acid on all they touch.

At every given juncture, we humans are given the freedom to choose the attitudes we assume, and so it was with me: I could be *angry* that Laura Lue had died after only ten short years; or I could be *grateful* that she had lived at all and that I had been able to share in her wonder. I chose then, and I still do, *the way of gratitude.* The vision that broke over me in the words, "You are the light of the world," contributed greatly to the making of that choice.

That same vision also possessed the power to help me overcome despair. The feeling that there is nothing left to live for can be utterly immobilizing. But once again, there is tremendous potency in the vision *vision of life as gift* of life as gift. After all, if God were generous enough and good enough to create the past, can he not be trusted to provide a meaningful future? Is it too much to expect that the One who authored "the good old days" will give us "good new days"? Such an attitude of hopeful expectancy calls for both flexibility and humility on our part.

There is a peril implicit in every strong human virtue, and the danger of great affection is that it may become idolatry. I have known people who were so attached to one individual or to a given set of circumstances that they would say, "If I cannot have her or him or that, I do not want anything else." Such rigidity will undermine the gift of a new future, as surely as will the unbelief that leads one to think that not even God could bring joy again into one's existence. When, however, human suppleness and trust are joined, the vision of life as gift can produce a Lazarus-like experience. For behold, he who can make things "that are out of things that are not" possesses an even greater creative power—he can give new life (hope) to the hopeless.

Such was my experience at the beginning of the 1970s, in the deepest abyss of sorrow and darkness I had ever known. But the sense that life is a gift—that it is God's creation, not something we ourselves have made—sustained me through that period of numbness. Slowly, like the coming of springtime, it called me back to vitality and aliveness. I saw that as precious as Laura Lue had been, she was not the only gift. There was also a son, and a natural world of wonder and beauty, and so many things to learn and experience and discover and do! Thus life flowed on, and I, like Jacob, though walking with a limp, moved on.

That decade proved to be eventful, although not as dramatic and intense as the 1960s. That was to be expected, I suppose. Daniel Levinson points out that following the upheavals of the mid-adult crisis when old value assessments are often laid aside and new life choices made, there comes a time of structure building, a time when the new vision is more fully assimilated and acted upon. And such was my experience.

The lessening of drivenness, of the need to make a name for myself, opened up new vistas of freedom. I was approached about becoming the pastor of a very prestigious church in another state, and as I considered my decision, I became distinctly aware that much within me had changed. There was considerable pressure from my peers to assume the post—it offered a kind of visibility one did not have in Kentucky. By the same token, deep within my own spirit I found no joy at the prospect. Flying back from an interview with the church's search committee, I realized that I no longer needed important offices or everyone's approval. To discover the gifts within and pass them on to others, to become a genuinely good and joyful human being— these were the goals that mattered to me now. Thus I turned down that offer on the basis of nothing more tangible than the feeling that it was not my "promised land." I later accepted a church with not nearly as much reknown, simply because I sensed within myself that it was "given." I was being drawn to it positively, rather than driven by negative emotions.

I want to emphasize again, however, that my growth in grace was erratic. The great discovery I made in the 1960s had to do with the worth and value that God had placed in the center of my being at the moment of my creation. It was exciting indeed to "see" for the first time the potential that "came with the territory"—the

the reality of limits

potential that was mine to discover and develop and give away. But my next lesson concerned another aspect of that giftedness—the reality of limits. No individual can mature until that person has begun to come to terms with all aspects of his or her being. One needs to know not only where one begins, but also where one must stop. What one *cannot* do is also an integral part of one's uniqueness. It was necessary for me to minister in a church that was openly innovative in order to learn the "limits" lesson.

The various sections of America do share deep commonalities, but there are differences as well. A move from an older part of the country—Kentucky— where precedent and tradition are powerful dynamics, to a younger section—Texas—where all is exuberant and full of energy, is quite a shift. I was newly liberated and less tense about my own capabilities, and the church in Texas was ready and willing to try any unusual adventure. It was a heady combination and made for some of the most exhilarating experiences of ministry I have known—except for one thing: I did not yet recognize the reality of limits.

Since recovering from my mid-adult crisis, I had not given much thought to the issue of fatigue. However, my experience in Texas brought that problem home to me inescapably. For all its pain, I am grateful now for the lesson. The catch is that fatigue can slip up on one gradually, almost imperceptibly. It is authentically Christian to want to enter fully into the creative opportunities that are all about—to desire to be part of the answer and not part of the problem. And that is what I was trying to do. But I was overlooking another important reality-principle—that *too much of any good thing becomes a bad thing.* This is true of food, exercise, sex—everything, in fact—even innovative Christian ministry. In time, my activities began to lose their savor. Problems began to loom larger than life, and resources to cope with them seemed insufficient. I felt like a water skier who has fallen off the skis but is still holding on to the rope. I was being dragged along through events in a way that was less than satisfying, to say the least!

[margin note: felt like a water skier.. dragged along..]

I finally became aware enough to recognize this condition as fatigue. Therefore when the opportunity to move to a much smaller church in the more staid Southeast presented itself, I rather impulsively decided to take advantage of it. Thus I arrived at Northminster Baptist Church in Jackson, Mississippi.

[margin note: fatigue]

Fatigue was a significant, but by no means the only factor that influenced my decision. The process that had begun with seeing worth in my own particularity was very much at work in propelling me another step toward what Abraham Maslow called self-actualization. For some years now, I had been learning to listen more and more to the still small voices within than to the many clamoring cries from without; I had been learning to trust that sense of rightness which wells up from the depths of one's own being. This had been increasingly leading me in the direction of ministry on a qualitative rather than a quantitative scale, to relationships with individuals rather than with masses.

Let me emphasize that this seems to be my own sense of calling. I am not attempting to make a normative statement for all Christian ministry. I know clergy who appear to possess the gift of ministering simultaneously to each person in a large group, and I applaud that gift. One such man said to me, "I love people by the acre, but cannot stand them one by one." I accept that attitude as being valid for him. But I must acknowledge that when I am true to my own feelings, I have just the opposite attitude! I relish interaction with individuals—at real depth if possible. It is those people-by-the-acre situations that drain me most and satisfy me least.

This predilection was not new; I had felt that way since the earliest days of my ministry. However, I was part of a national and denominational culture that maintains a very different hierarchy of values: Southern Baptists have taken over the American bigger-is-better ideal, hook, line, and sinker. And so, for years, I had sacrificed my preference in order to win the approval of others—to make it big with that particular audience. I had made every effort to obtain a large church; I had invested sixteen vigorous years in attempting to make that form of ministry work. But it was never a good fit, to use Daniel Levinson's phrase. I had never liked the superficiality of relationships that are inherent in that way of doing church. To preach to people when I did not even know their names, much less their innermost beings and struggles; to conduct funerals and weddings for virtual strangers; to be unable to thoroughly discuss the concerns of individuals—that was simply not the shape of my particular joy.

By 1976, however, the movement from acquisition to awareness had developed to a point where I was able to set my own sense of reality against the imposed culture. Thus I took an unthinkable action for a Southern Baptist (or for an American). I voluntarily moved from large to small—from a church of some 5,000 members to one of 450. It proved to be the wisest move I ever made.

That is not to say that it was the easiest or the most satisfying move, in the beginning. I had not realized until then how much I still craved the approval of others. Much of the change that C. S. Lewis once thought had taken place in his life proved to be largely imaginary, he said. "The real work is still to be done." *"still to be done"* That was my experience also, and I believe it reconfirms the process-character of human experience. I was not then and still am not by any means out of the old ways and into the new. But I had grown in awareness of the worth within to some extent, or I never could have moved so against the stream. I used to hear Martin Luther King, Jr., close many of his talks with the old slave's prayer: "O God, I ain't what I ought to be and I ain't what I'm gonna be, but thanks be to you, I ain't what I used to be!" The best we humans can hope for is incremental growth—we can never arrive at total perfection. The move to Jackson and the opportunity for more authentic ministry according to my own lights was satisfying in that sense. *MLK: old slave's prayer*

One other aspect of my past faith-journey is worthy of mention before I turn toward the future. It pertains to my understanding of God and the actions involved in relating to God. It should be obvious that the movement from acquisition to awareness can be fraught with theological as well as personal implications. My earliest images of God, as well as of myself—not surprisingly—were decidedly negative. God was The Great Killjoy, the enemy of all happiness, the One to whom one finally "surrendered" and *changing images of God* thereafter lived a life of drabness and sacrifice (becoming a missionary to Africa was a likely fate). The love of such a One must be earned, of course, by strenuous effort. Obviously I was as mistaken about God as I was about myself, and an exciting dimension of my grace pilgrimage has been that I see God differently and am learning to relate to Transcendence in light of this new vision.

My perception of God has changed as much as has my sense of self. I now see God as joy and generosity. For example, I can imagine that long ago, finding aliveness so joyful a reality, God said, "This is too good to keep to myself. I want others to feel some of this ecstasy. I know what I shall do: I shall create—not to *receive* anything *for* myself, but to *give* something *of* myself." Thus Creation was an act of bottomless sharing! That is the Ground of Being, to use Paul Tillich's famous term, out of which all creation was formed and continues "to live and move and have its being."

From these visions, it follows that a relationship with such a God becomes one of trust and discernment, rather than placation and manipulation. Thus my prayer life is another area that has undergone a significant transformation. Before my encounter with grace, prayer was largely a matter of making my requests known to God, trying to enlist God's aid, using God as a means to attain the ends that I had in mind. Prayer was just another effort in the process of acquisition. As I became more and more reconciled to the goodness and wisdom and mystery of God, however, the focus shifted, and with it, even the way I go about prayer. Now I have become a means for the attaining of God's ends, rather than the other way around. I attempt to empty myself and silence myself sufficiently so that what God wants to give and say can be received and heard.

I have come to regard prayer much more as an experience of meeting than as a time of requesting. I find great excitement in literally "waiting upon the Lord," allowing configurations of meanings that are often surprising, but nonetheless real, to rise up from the depths within or descend from the heights above. Thus listening and discerning have become as much a part of my prayer routine as asking and seeking and knocking. I will have more to say about this later. I include it here to illustrate the fundamental nature of the movement from acquisition to awareness.

The transforming work is by no means completed, but already there is no facet of my being—from my image of God and of myself to the way I work and sleep and pray—that has not been touched by the ripple effect of that incredible discovery: I have worth by God's grace and do not need to earn it. What better good news could there be?

PART TWO: LOOKING AHEAD

6

Opening Blind Eyes
to Self-Worth

The invitation to participate in this series was twofold—to reflect upon the faith-journey of the 1960s and 1970s and, out of those learnings, to look ahead to the 1980s, identifying those challenges that seem to be most seminal for the church. I have described the most important change experience in my life during those years—the shift from acquisition to awareness—and I have said that the work of salvation is still going on. What does this perspective suggest, then, for the ministry of the church in the decade ahead?

If the image of a person riding on an ox, looking for an ox describes our human situation, it follows that the image of opening blind eyes must describe the solution. In my judgment, the church's task is not to create certain realities that do not exist, but to make people aware of what already exists but has not been recognized. Thomas Merton called this recognition the breakthrough to the Already—one of the crucial moments in the process of redemption. I would apply this insight to the four primary relationships of existence: relation to the individual self; relation to God; relation to other human beings; and relation to society, humankind collectively. The great challenge before the church in the 1980s is to find ways to participate with the risen Christ in a *ministry of awakening* on all levels—personal, transcendent, relational, and societal.

I feel strongly that the church should invest significant energy in ministry to individuals—be concerned with the way they image themselves, feel about themselves. This is a foundational sector of human experience. I agree with the old dictum that "if religion stops with the individual, it stops—period." But the other side of that truth is that if religion does not begin with the individual, it will not begin at all. The way one decides to view oneself is crucial to all subsequent experiences. My seminary teacher, Wayne Oates, was the first to point this out to me. Jesus' famous dictum "You shall love your neighbor as yourself," he said, was as much a statement of psychological fact as an ethical imperative. "You *will* love your neighbor as you love yourself. The pattern you develop in relating to the very first person you ever encounter lays down the tracks for the way you relate to everyone else."

This idea was reinforced for me many years later when transactional analysis began to receive attention in the church. During an all-day workshop in Fort Worth, our instructor illustrated this point with a spectrum—a big circle, with ten positions, five on each side, fanning out from it. On the right side, the first position was titled "I'm OK"; position two, "You're OK"; position three, "We're OK"; position four, "They're OK"; position five, "It's OK." The five positions on the other side of the circle bore comparable negative labels—"I'm *not* OK," and so on. The point is that everything depends on the way one moves out of the circle in relation to oneself. If the starting assumption is negative—I'm not OK—that sets the tone for all other perceptions: Other individuals will be regarded negatively; one's "in groups" and "out groups," and finally, all of reality itself will be swallowed up in negativity and dissatisfaction. By the same token, if one is able to affirm one's own existence and accept "the way it is" as positive, that will become the basis of affirming other individuals, other groups, and eventually the whole sweep of reality.

Karen Horney, a great pioneer in the whole area of neurotic behavior, made the same point. She traced this malfunction of spirit to a condition she called basic anxiety about one's self—the feeling that somehow one does not belong, that one has no right to be here, that one is seriously inadequate. Such a conclusion has a way of coloring all subsequent perceptions. Rudolph Dreikurs, one of Horney's followers, put it this way:

> A sense of security is only possible if one is sure of his place, sure of his ability to cope with whatever may come, and sure of his worth and value. Anyone who believes he must energetically seek his place will never find it. He does not know that by his mere presence he already does belong and has a place. If one has to be more than he is in order to be somebody, he will never be anybody. If one does not realize

that he is good enough as he is, he will never have any reason
to assume that he is good enough, regardless of how much
money, power, superiority . . . he may amass. It is obvious
that in our society few people believe they are good enough
as they are, and can therefore be sure of their esteemed
place. Everyone tries to be more, to be better, to reach
higher, and as a consequence, we are all neurotic, in a
neurotic society which pays a premium to the over-ambitious
search for prestige and striving for superiority. . . . Under-
neath we are all frightened people, not sure of ourselves, of
our worth, or of our place. It is this doubt of oneself,
expressed in a feeling of inadequacy and inferiority, which
. . . is at the root of all maladjustment and psychopathology
(*Concepts of Personality*, ed. Joseph Wepman and Ralph
Heine).

I believe this is an accurate reflection, not only of the
importance of self-image, but also of the cultural
milieu in which most of us in the western world live out
our lives. My own story, which I traced earlier, is an
excellent illustration. Society drives us relentlessly to
succeed and achieve, but it provides no source of
energy for our efforts. The gospel offers a perspective
on reality that is radically different from the neurotic
striving that results from a sense of emptiness, and no
other perspective is more relevant to pressured, urban
Americans in the 1980s.

In order to work effectively in this area, the church
must have a clear grasp of the whole process of
self-imaging, and of ways to unlearn and relearn at this
profound psychic level. The problem is often a
consequence of the fact that small children's powers of
observation exceed their abilities of interpretation.
They have so little experience on which to base their
reasoning that they often come to very false conclusions.

children's interpretation, primal images

Myron Madden has illustrated this tendency in relation to the phenomenon of death. Children observe death very concretely and literally—a puppy is alive one minute, then is hit by an automobile and, for all practical purposes, simply is no more. It is the same when grandparents or other human beings die—for the child, they completely disappear. Thus the child concludes that death is an annihilator of all it touches. When this image is internalized in the depths of a human psyche, it is no wonder that an irrational fear of death develops, with all its accompanying disorders. And until that image is replaced by the more positive image of death as an experience of transition and growth, the whole psyche will continue to be affected.

This process which Madden has described in relation to the idea of death pertains also to everything else in a child's experience. In the celebrated movie *Kramer vs. Kramer,* the little boy had pressed his father beyond endurance in order to eat some forbidden ice cream. An angry scene had resulted, and in its aftermath, one of the most touching moments occurred: The seven-year-old asked his father, "Are you going to leave me, too, like Mama did?" The child assumed that his mother had abandoned the family because of his bad behavior. The truth was something very different. Her departure had nothing to do with the child's behavior; it had to do only with the woman's own search for identity. Here again, we see that children are keen observers but poor interpreters. They take it all in, but are often mistaken in their conclusions.

Such primal images, however, whether true or false, are powerful influences. An illusion can have as much psychic potency as actuality. If the ministry of "opening the eyes of the blind" is to be effective at the point of self-image, the church must understand clearly how such images are formed and how they develop. Then it must ask: How can we return to those places where erroneous conclusions were formed and help individuals unlearn and relearn at that level, so that their lives are governed by actuality, not illusion?

My great mentor, Carlyle Marney, describes the returning-and-relearning process as the courage "to submit to the group my images of me to be corrected by the highest that we know—Jesus, the Christ." He maintains that this process should be at the heart of all religious education programs offered by the church. I agree. Rather than dispersing bits of information about biblical facts, the church must create structures of loving interaction in which people are encouraged and enabled to bring their images up out of the murky waters of unconsciousness, so that they may be updated and reshaped by the Spirit of God amid a community of concerned brothers and sisters. In this way the devastating spell of illusion and erroneous fantasy can be broken, and human beings can be literally set free to perceive all things more positively.

Such a task will require a great deal of love and competence and mercy and patience. Unlearning and relearning cannot be accomplished all at once or without effort or sacrifice. The story Jesus told about the prodigal son is archetypal, in my judgment, of this challenge that faces the church—to help people to a positive sense of self-worth.

It is obvious at the beginning of the prodigal's story that this younger son, for all his keen observation, was

in fact poor at interpretation. He knew very little about
himself, about his family, or about the world at large.
In particular, he was unaware of his limits. He had
grandiose ideas about his potential and about what he
could accomplish, and this led him to do a thing that
was at once arrogant and highly insensitive. He asked
for his share of the inheritance so that he might leave
his dreary home and go out and bend reality to his own
liking. It was arrogant because it implied that he could
live life better than anyone at home had been able to
live it. It was insensitive because it was saying, in effect,
"Father, I wish you were dead. I wish that this were the
day after your funeral and we were dividing up what is
left." But interestingly enough, the old man was wise
enough and tough enough in his love to let the boy go
and learn for himself what he refused to be taught. So
without delay, the prodigal took his inheritance and
headed for the "far country."

There, almost immediately, the lad collided head-
on with reality. Paul Tillich describes reality as "what
we have to adjust to because we discover it will not
adjust to us." It did not take the prodigal long to find
out that he was not nearly as smart or as powerful as he
had thought, nor was life as responsive to his wishes as
he had supposed. Before long, he had lost his whole
inheritance.

When a famine struck the land, he—Jewish lad that
he was—was reduced to having to tend pigs. In a word,
the prodigal had become "demythologized"—all the
grandiose images of himself were shattered, and he
came face to face with the fact of his limits: He could
not do everything. It was a stunning revelation, but it
was the beginning of a process that Jesus describes as

"coming to himself." For the first time, the boy really began to be aware of life the way it really is.

That is what Christian redemption is all about. We do not need to seek somewhere else or acquire something else—we need only become aware of what already is. There in the pigpen, the prodigal was setting out on the journey from illusion to actuality, that important "rite of passage."

My former colleague Anne Davis, with whom I served in Louisville and who now teaches at Southern Baptist Theological Seminary, used to say that the temptation experiences of Jesus were his rites of passage from childhood and adolescence into adulthood. Each of the temptations was in fact the kind of fantasy every child has. Turn stones into bread—what child has not wished that, at a snap of the fingers, a piece of cake would instantly materialize? Jump off the pinnacle of the Temple—what child has not wished to do away with the law of gravity or the restrictions of space, to be at one place this moment and a hundred miles away the next? What child has not dreamed of having the whole world presented on a platter? So Jesus was grappling then, Davis pointed out, with the adjustment we all must face when we let go the fantasies that are part of childhood. He was dealing with life as it is. In each case, Jesus opted for actuality over fantasy—for a world in which one must sow and reap and grind and bake in order to have bread, a world in which one must walk up steps and put forth some effort.

Jesus successfully negotiated those rites of passage, as did the prodigal when he began to realize that he did have limits, that he was not totally omnipotent.

Would the boy ever have come to that self-understanding without those harsh interactions with reality? No one can be sure, but such confrontation is often a real aspect of Christian redemption.

When our main concern is to shield people from pain, we will produce little more than hothouse plants who cannot make it in the real world. Much of the truth that becomes existentially our own grows out of our wounds. The father's willingness to let the prodigal go stands out as an important lesson for the church in developing redemptive structures. There is a key tenet in my proposals for religious education in the 1980s: *Only the truth can bless!* A crucial ingredient must be the tough love that is able to deny people ease and contentment so that they may experience growth in self-understanding.

But of course, that is not all that needs to be done, as our archetypal parable so clearly suggests. The prodigal did not outgrow all his illusions, once he began to become more aware. In fact, he did what most people do: He went from one extreme to the other. Martin Luther once compared the human being to a drunken peasant who falls off his horse on one side, only to mount again and fall off on the other. And this is what the prodigal did: He who once had believed he had no limits at all now concluded that he had no potential. He who once had imaged himself as a superman now saw himself only as a hired servant. He who had demanded total freedom now wanted no freedom at all. The father, who had seemed the epitome of dullness a short time before, now looked very appealing as an absolute authority. So with a great

from illusion to another illusion

desire to reenter the womb psychologically—to become an infant again—the prodigal headed back
home. There, phase two of his redemption/awakening
was accomplished.

In my judgment, the father in the parable is both an
image of God and an image of those who work with
God in finishing creation. The key here is knowing
how to facilitate maturity—how to open the eyes of the
blind and unmask illusions. First the father was wise
enough to let the prodigal learn what he refused to be
taught. Now he shows he is strong enough not to allow
the prodigal to return on the infantile terms the son is
requesting. After the boy blurted out his words of
shame and guilt and impotence, the father took him by
the shoulders and turned him around. Instead of a
bassinet, the father called for a ring, a robe, and
shoes—symbols of authority and power. He invited
the lad to accept the identity that always had been his,
but which until that moment he had steadfastly
denied. The boy was not a superman, as his experience
in the far country had so vividly taught him, but
neither was he a hired servant. He was a son, a resident
of the manor house, a junior partner in the enterprise
of the family business. Here was his true identity, the
"ox" on which he had been riding from the beginning.
Coming home was yet another stage in opening his
eyes to what was already there. In the far country, he
had come to terms with the reality of his limits. Now he
was challenged to come to terms with the strengths
that existed within his own being and to learn to use
them responsibly.

Another image of this same process is contained in a
fable told by the Hindu saint Ramakrishna in the

nineteenth century. It seems that the mother of a tiger cub was killed shortly after he was born, and the little fellow fell in with a herd of wild goats. Predictably, he adopted all their ways. (All creatures are conditioned by their environment.) One day, King Tiger happened along, and he asked the young tiger the meaning of this unseemly masquerade. But the cub could only bleat nervously and nibble at the grass. The little animal had no idea what he was. So King Tiger took the little tiger down to a stream and let him look at his reflection for the first time, alongside that of the large tiger. "Here is what you were meant to be," King Tiger said. "You are not a goat. You are a tiger. You were not born to eat grass or to bleat as goats do. Here is some raw meat—eat it. Here is how you are supposed to sound." And with that, King Tiger threw back his head and roared. In that moment the young tiger's eyes were opened. He saw what he was—what he had always been—and he accepted King Tiger's invitation to follow him into the jungle, to learn how to become all that he was meant to be. *became what he was*

That is exactly what the father did for the prodigal. The secret lay in inducing the prodigal to become aware of what already was, rather than to feel the need to acquire something he did not have. He did not suddenly become the son of his father when he awakened to his true identity. He had always been that son. But in that moment, his eyes were opened to this ox on which he had been riding all his days. At last his illusions were unmasked and he saw and accepted actuality as it always had been. *illusions unmasked at last*

At a functional level, this must be one of the meanings of the term *born again*. I believe it refers to the process in which the risen Christ goes all the way back into our lives, into those places where we have made erroneous judgments, and there he helps us relearn ourselves.

The Book of Genesis states clearly that all creation comes out of the joyous intention of God. If one looks carefully at the statements in Genesis 1, it is obvious that God had no need to create. But God found aliveness so joyful that it must be shared. "This is too good to keep," God must have said. So generosity, not acquisition, became the primal motive for creation.

Genesis then pictures God as carrying through this resolve, and at every stage, looking at the work and saying, "It is good, good—very, very, good." This image in the Hebrew is very primitive—that of a child who looks on something with relish and exclaims, "Look! Look! It is good. It is good. It is very, very good!" *The goal of Christian redemption is to induce us to feel about the event of our creation the way God is pictured as feeling; and to enable us to celebrate our actuality the way God is depicted as celebrating it.*

This, it seems to me, is what the prodigal began to realize after his pilgrimage through illusion. He saw, then, not only the value of his own personhood, but the incredible mercy of his father, who had waited patiently through all those years. There is real pathos in the words the lad had spoken: "I am no longer worthy to be called your son." What could be worse than finally to recognize a certain truth, only to believe that the things one had done have now cut one off from that truth? But the prodigal now saw that what he had not had a part in creating, he could not destroy! The boy had not become the son of his father by some act of worthiness, and he could not destroy that relationship by being unworthy. As Sam Keen learned, it comes with the territory.

Thus our relationship to God is not finally the result of what we do or do not do. It is the result of what God has done. We can deny it, we can distort it, we can refuse to make that relationship the functional basis of our living, but there is nothing we can do to break the bond that binds us to God.

In relation to self-image, then, the challenge of the church is to open blind eyes to two realities: a true image of self; and the mercy that gives us life apart from our deserving—not once, but again and again. What a gospel this is! What a privilege to work to unmask illusions and enable people to "come to themselves" and to the mercy that will not let them go, that never gives up, and that celebrates whenever and however blind eyes are finally opened.

7

Relating
to the Ultimate

Many in this century have observed that the scientifically trained, secularly oriented human being finds it difficult to experience the realm of the Transcendent. Despite all we in the West have gained in the last four centuries, we seem to have lost the ability to relate meaningfully and personally to the God-reality. No doubt the great interest in Eastern religions and disciplines of meditation and contemplation that has so gripped Americans recently is a sign of this perceived lack and an attempt to do something about it.

What is our basic difficulty? I believe it is another manifestation of unawareness. Early in life, when our powers of observation exceeded our powers of interpretation, we came to certain conclusions about the Divine One and about the way we should relate to that Divinity. To the degree that those conclusions are false, they lead us into greater and greater unreality.

Erich Heller, in *The Disinherited Mind*, related an episode which supplies a graphic image for our plight:

> The late Munich comedian, Karl Vallentin—one of the greatest of the rare race of metaphysical clowns—once enacted the following scene: the curtain goes up and reveals darkness; and in this darkness is a solitary circle of light thrown by a street-lamp. Vallentin, with his long-drawn and deeply worried face, walks round and round this circle of light, desperately looking for something. "What have you lost?" a policeman asks who has entered the scene. "The key to my house." Upon which the policeman joins him in his search; they find nothing; and after a while he inquires: "Are you sure you lost it here?" "No," says Vallentin, and pointing to a dark corner of the stage: "Over there." "Then why on earth are you looking for it here?" "There is no light over there," says Vallentin.

looking for something where it does not exist

Is this not akin to riding on an ox, looking for an ox? When one looks for something in a place where it does not exist, one's efforts are doomed to failure. This is one of the problems that inhibits our relationship to God—our expectations are in error. More often than not, disillusion is the child of illusion—if one begins with a false set of assumptions, false conclusions are bound to follow.

The church must face this issue squarely in the 1980s, if authentic relations with God are to be established and enjoyed. People must unlearn and relearn at the deepest level—the movement from acquisition to awareness here is as crucial here as in other areas.

The witness of biblical revelation can be highly instructive, for it suggests that the single most important word used to describe God is *holy*. This

"holy"

word has come to have a largely moralistic connotation, but the original Hebrew comes from a root word meaning *to be separate* and thus stands for the utter uniqueness of the divine Reality. God is literally incomparable, the Only-One-of-a-Kind. There is nothing else exactly like God.

Christian philosophers have long declared that there are only two final orders of reality in the world: the uncreated form—that which has life in itself and gives life to others; and the created forms—those which derive their existence from another. It follows that only God rightly belongs to the uncreated order, and everything else belongs to the created order. The functional implication of this philosophy is that an experience with God will never be exactly like the experience with anything else we encounter. There may be similarities, but if God really is the Holy One, the Only-One-of-a-Kind, then it follows that surprise and uniqueness will characterize our interactions with the Ultimate.

Again and again the sophomores of this world have said, "God never has spoken to me. I never have seen or touched God." Such statements imply that God should be exactly like some created part of the universe. This is an error in expectation that must be unlearned if the Ultimate is to be experienced as it really is. If we construct our own images of God and interpret our experience through such expectations, we may miss God altogether. The appropriate stance in relation to the Holy One is utter openness and flexibility and high sensitivity. We humans must prepare for God's coming with silence, emptiness, and receptivity.

To me, God is the Holy One whose other name is Surprise. The willingness to let the Ultimate assume whatever form he will and come in whatever manner *i the* chooses is absolutely crucial, and it must be coupled with our trust that God wants to become known to us and is able to communicate with us, if we will allow it on those terms. That is the way authentic experience with the biblical God occurs. We do not create it or acquire it by our own efforts; we only respond to that which is graciously given—in a form we might never have anticipated, but that nonetheless is there.

I had to learn this the same way I learned the truth about my worth—through decades of unsuccessfully attempting to acquire it by my own efforts.

Though I was born and raised in an intensely religious atmosphere, by the time I was ten years old I had learned that there were other options than the one into which I had been born. For example, a real live atheist moved in up the street from us, and his son became my closest playmate. My friend said that *his* father thought that anyone who believes there is a God is a plain fool. I was stunned and frightened by such talk in my own front yard. It was utterly different from everything I had always heard *my* father say. But when I asked myself, "How do you *know* his father is wrong and yours is right?" I realized I had no answer. At that point, my religious conclusions were merely shadows cast by my parents' beliefs. Even though I was young, I sensed clearly that such second-hand faith could not survive in a world as complex and varied as I was discovering ours to be. *atheist*

Later, when I became acquainted with an Iranian exchange student, that sense of multiple options was *Moslem* intensified as I heard for the first time of the Koran—a book, incidentally, that looked for all the world like our Holy Bible, except that it was very different—God was called Allah there, not Jehovah, and its prophet was not named Jesus, but Muhammad. Then, too, I had an older friend who went to college and began taking philosophy courses. He came home asking questions and raising issues I had never considered before, but which boggled my mind.

When the vastness of the world began to shatter the simplicity of my innocence, I went straight to God in prayer and asked, "Who are you, God?" Like Jacob by the brook Jabbok, I tried by my own efforts to wrest God's secret from him. "Mystery, mystery, what is your name?" I demanded. I still remember the awesome silence that followed that impassioned adolescent request. For some eight years I pushed and pleaded and begged. I really wanted to know both the truth about God (was it Allah or Jehovah or Who?) and God personally, if that were possible. But my own efforts to "make God happen" came to naught. The terms *silence of God, absence of God,* and even *death of God* are existential realities to me, for I know what it is like *not to know.* And then it happened—that same movement from acquisition to awareness that later became so basic to my experience.

When I entered Mars Hill College I had the great good fortune to meet a professor of religion who understood my dilemma. Instead of heaping scorn upon me for having questions and doubts, he encouraged me to relax, to open the windows of my being, and to let *truth* find *me,* rather than thinking that *I* had to find the *truth.* He gave me a copy of a book that

had just come out—J. B. Phillips' *Your God Is Too Small.*
I became fascinated by the way Phillips identified false
images of God and then argued for incarnational
Christianity, quoting extensively from the Fourth
Gospel.

I recall that I laid aside the volume, picked up the
Bible, and began to read from John's prologue: "In
the beginning was the Word, and the Word was with
God, and the Word was God. . . . And the Word was
made flesh, and dwelt among us." Then suddenly, it
was as if in total darkness a light had begun to shine. I
had been alone, but now I felt another's presence, and
there welled up inside me a profound realization of
truth! The face of the Ultimate was the face of Jesus!
Now at last I knew the reality of God!

I cannot tell you how surprised I was. This was not
anything I had planned. To be perfectly honest, it was
not what I wanted at that particular moment. I was
involved, you see, in a good bit of adolescent rebellion,
and nothing would have pleased the rebel in me more
than to go home a Hindu, or a Buddhist, or dressed in
the orange gown of a Hare Krishna follower. On the
night that God finally made himself known to C. S.
Lewis, he was the most dejected convert in all England.
You see, Lewis did not want an Ultimate Authority
laying claim to every last particle of his being. That was
pretty much my mind-set, too. Nevertheless, God
happened to me that day, and the event's givenness so
encompassed me that I could not mistake it for my
own creation.

Had God appeared to me years before when I had
demanded a sign, I might well have concluded that the
Ultimate is some kind of cosmic bellhop who comes

and goes according to one's bidding. But all that asking and seeking and knocking were futile. I could not make God come on my terms. It was not until I relaxed and let God come on his own terms that I was conscious of his presence. It was akin to the prodigal's "coming to himself," Merton's "breakthrough to the Already." My eyes were opened, and I realized that God had always been with me, but I had not perceived him. I became aware of him because I finally saw what already was, rather than what I thought must be acquired.

what was already was

This is the best wisdom I have gained concerning the all-important question of facilitating religious experience. We get into trouble because of the images of God which we constructed early in life. The best images of God are no images at all—except the sure realization that, although utterly unpredictable, God desires and is able to make contact with us. When we "let go" and learn the discipline of honest contemplation, we set the stage for this surprising One to come. How God will do it—that is uncertain. But God can do it and will do it—that is certain!

Charles Haddon Spurgeon discovered this fact early in his life and it became the foundation of his ministry. As an adolescent, he had become convinced of his own sinfulness and unworthiness. He went from church to church, desperately seeking ways to earn God's favor and work his way into God's forgiveness. One Sunday morning he had attended a little Methodist chapel. The service was delayed, and finally it became obvious that the circuit rider would not be there that day. Spurgeon was disappointed and on the verge of leaving, but then an old layman arose, turned to the Book of Isaiah, and began to read: "Look unto me, ye ends of the earth and be saved." And suddenly Spurgeon realized that all God asks us to do is *look*—to become aware of what already is. It is not by earning, but by receiving that the Mystery of Godness becomes the Reality.

This is another of the church's challenges in the 1980s—to point the way for scientifically trained, secularly oriented people to experience the Divine. That experience is found by "looking unto him"—by awareness. In this way, the Mystery happens to us and will continue to happen.

not earning, but receiving

8

Relating to Significantly Other Others

I believe that unawareness is *the* problem in the religious realm, that awakening is *the* answer and therefore the basic challenge of Christian ministry. We all are riding on an ox, looking for an ox. There are certain things about Reality that already exist, but most of us do not recognize them. We are asleep and unaware, in the clutch of illusion and false images. Thus the great challenge to the church lies not in persuading people to strain and struggle to acquire something they do not possess, but rather in opening their eyes to what *does* exist. Such awakening is the epitome of a religion of grace, as opposed to a religion of law.

Think about it for a moment. Legalistic religions, in whatever form they may exist, concentrate on what one must earn or achieve or acquire by one's own efforts. A religion of grace focuses on what is given; it calls on one to discern, accept, perceive, and begin to live out of that bounty. Throughout its history, Christianity has had its bouts with legalism, but at its core, it is a religion of grace. What God does and gives—not what we humans do and achieve—is the essence of the good news.

Now we reach the third relational category—our images of other human beings. Here once again, the answer does not lie in attempting to acquire something we do not possess. It lies in washing the lens of our perception so that we can see what other people already are and thus begin to act accordingly.

One night during the Middle Ages, two warriors in full armor were riding along, each thinking there was no one else for miles around. They happened upon each other at a particularly dark spot. Both were startled and each misinterpreted the movements of the other as gestures of hostility. So they began to fight, each believing he was under attack and must defend himself. The conflict grew more intense until one knight finally succeeded in unhorsing the other. Then, with one mighty effort, he drove his lance through the fallen man's heart. The victor dismounted and limped over to the adversary he had just killed. He pulled back the face mask, and there to his horror, in the pale moonlight, he recognized his own brother! He had mistaken a kinsman for an enemy and had destroyed him!

I would like to suggest that one of the ministries of the church in the 1980s must be to find ways to reverse the process that leads to such human tragedy. Instead of seeing others as enemies and moving to destroy them—largely the story of our planet—our goal should be to open people's eyes so that they see others as kinspeople. The Christian ethic is rooted in a faith deeper than "oughts" and "shoulds." The question is crucial: What do we *see* as we look upon another human being? What image do we have of the other, of how and why that other came to be here? More than anything else, this will control the way we relate to one another.

Something the late Ralph Sockman said is appropriate here. He declared that we humans actually have been given three mechanisms of perception. First there are the eyes of the body, those intricate organs through which we perceive the shapes and outer surfaces of realities. With these particular eyes, we see form and color and outward manifestations.

In addition to the eyes of the body, we have been equipped, Sockman says, with the eyes of the mind. This capacity organizes all the data that flow in through our senses into patterns of meaning and understanding. The eyes of the mind link past and present experience, so that we possess insight, something very different from visual ability. We can make a connection, we can put the pieces of a puzzle together in new configurations of meaning. Insight distinguishes the human species from animal and plant life, but it does not exhaust our giftedness.

Sockman also identifies what he calls the eyes of the heart. The eyes of the body relate to *what* a particular object is. The eyes of the mind relate to *how* a bit of information fits together with everything else we know. But the eyes of the heart search for the final understanding: *Why* has this thing come to be?

Paul Tillich says that a single question launched him on his philosophic career—the question every child

has asked: Why something and not nothing? Here we
reach the ultimate dimension: Why does anything
exist at all? And this, of course, is where we encounter
the Divine.

With the eyes of the heart, we begin to see that
"everything that is, is because of God." The only
reason anything *exists*—the word literally means *to
stand out from nothingness*—is the fact that God wanted it
to be and has given it life. Between awesome
nothingness and existence, there is a single creative
link—God. Thus if we look long enough and intensely
enough, using all the faculties of sight we have been
given, we will finally see "all things in God and God in
all things." God is the Fount from which all creation
flows. That realization can literally transform the way
we regard a thing or a person. To see through that
thing and that person as if they were transparent, all
the way back to their Source, is to see them in a
different light. I firmly believe that Christian ethics
will never be more than a conceptual or legalistic game
until we open people's eyes to the reality of other
people.

When that is accomplished, all kinds of other
changes can take place. And that is when the process
that led to the tragedy of the two knights can be
reversed. While we perceive one another as enemies,
destruction follows. But when we can live at the
deepest level of which we are capable—the contemplative level, where we utilize not only the eyes of the
body and the mind, but the eyes of the heart as well—
when we can perceive one another as kindred, then
the very opposite can occur. There will be no illusion
or distortion, and all danger of destruction can be

[margin note, handwritten:] Seeing God in Creation existence

avoided. The way we see others does make a
difference in our behavior.

I have heard it said that all sin grows out of a lack of
reverence. Years ago, Archbishop William Temple
declared that "war breaks out when worship breaks
down." To be honest, when I first read that statement,
I thought, "Here is the arrogance of a high churchman, claiming an ultimate significance for his particular enthusiasm." But I realize now that Temple was
right. Our tendency in the field of Christian ethics has
been to work too superficially. We have attempted to
formulate rules and govern behavior solely through
the eyes of the body and the eyes of the mind, and
these never penetrate deeply enough. Our behavior is
a result of our vision. It follows that if any of our "eyes"
are blinded or unused, we will see amiss and thus
behave in inauthentic ways.

This is the whole theme, it seems to me, of Jesus'
celebrated parable of the last judgment, in which he
tells his disciples that the whole human race will be
brought together and that judgment will be passed
both on those who have fulfilled their purpose in life
and on those who have missed it (Matt. 25:31-46). The
images are quite familiar: Those on the right are
pronounced "blessed" and are invited to enter into the
joy of their Lord; those on the left are judged as having
missed the whole point of their existence.

But what was the criterion for separation? It had to
do with how much or how little each group had *seen!*
Those on the right obviously had learned to utilize all
their capacities of sight—the eyes of the body, of the
mind, and of the heart. And because of their complete
sight, those people had been moved to respond to the

sick, the hungry, the naked, the imprisoned, the
outcast. They had seen beneath surface appearances
to the Ultimate dimension—where all persons are in
God and God is in all persons.

Those on the left, however, had seen only with the
eyes of the body and of the mind. When they
encountered individuals, they noted simply the outer
appearance, or they came to certain conclusions in
terms of attractiveness or utility. It never occurred to
those people to look more deeply—to ask: Where did
these individuals come from? To whom do they
ultimately belong? In what sense are we kindred
because we come from the same Source? They failed
to see the deepest truth—that those individuals were
their own brothers and sisters.

This really is the crucial issue—what we see or fail to
see. I remember that when I was dating a particular
girl, one of my friends asked, "What do you see in
her?" Obviously, there was a dimension of attractiveness which I perceived that he did not. I have often
thought that from an ethical standpoint, the question
What do you see in that person? ultimately controls the
way one responds and acts.

In G. K. Chesterton's beautiful little biography of
Francis of Assisi, he traces that remarkable ministry to
a moment of crucial awakening at the deepest levels of
Francis' being. The son of a wealthy merchant, Francis
wanted to become a poet and a warrior, but during one
of the military campaigns of his city-state, he became ill
and had to limp home in disgrace. His adolescent
vision of grandeur in utter shambles, he underwent
what must have been a rather serious episode of
personal depression: He went into a cave and

St Francis, 2
whes in cave

remained there alone for almost two weeks. But there "the breakthrough to the Already" occurred.

I believe that in that cave, Francis was led back to the beginning of things. He went, as it were, to the other side and glimpsed, with the eyes of his heart, the Source of creation. Thus Chesterton describes Francis as coming out of the cave "walking on his hands"—that is, he saw everything from a new perspective. When one is on one's feet, castles and trees seem to sit solidly on their own, as if they existed in their own right. However, when one stands on one's head, the same things appear literally to be hanging, the way a chandelier hangs by its chain.

What Francis discovered, says Chesterton, is that everything "hangs," or depends, on God. God is in all things and all things are in God. This was the secret of Francis' incredible power to affirm all that he encountered. He spoke affectionately to the birds and even to the trees—there was no particle of creation to which he did not feel a kinship. Why? Because the eyes of his heart had been opened to the fact that all is miracle because all is of God. Francis acted as he did because he saw as he did, and that kind of vision accounts for the remarkable Franciscan spirit.

Sight through the eyes of the heart is available to us as well. That is why I say that the ethical task of the Church is not to formulate rules, attempting to govern behavior authoritatively, but to make human beings aware of the three sets of eyes they already possess—to persuade them to open and use those eyes. Worship and reverence are the ground from which ethical behavior springs, and when we recognize that order of reality, we will have taken a great step toward revitalizing the ethical dimension of our ministry.

This whole perspective actually is foundational to our western view of reality. Years ago, as I waited at a red light in downtown Louisville, I noted the urban drama unfolding around me. In the lane to my right was a huge trailer truck, hauling several thousand pounds of merchandise. In the lane to my left was a brand new Cadillac, the finest model Detroit was then putting out. On each of the four corners was a valuable piece of commercial real estate. And limping across the street was one of the most pathetic looking human beings I have ever seen. The woman was old and appeared dissipated. Obviously, she had had a stroke—one side of her mouth drooped, and one foot was dragging behind the other. Her clothes were little more than dirty rags.

As I watched her, I asked myself, "If you were driving up to this corner and suddenly realized that your brakes were not working and you were going to hit something, which of these objects would you sacrifice in order to save the rest?" It did not take me two seconds to formulate an answer—I knew that I would hit any one of those other objects in order to avoid that human being. After all, I am a product of western civilization, and one of our cardinal tenets is that persons are of greater value than material objects.

However, as I drove away, I questioned myself further: "Why? On what basis does this particular value-judgment rest?" The judgment obviously was not grounded in aesthetics; by any standard one might have chosen, the human being was by no means the most beautiful of all the objects at that corner. Neither was it grounded on productivity or utilitarianism; any one of those pieces of real estate would have generated more income in a year than that woman could have earned in a lifetime, and she certainly could not do the work of a tractor-trailer rig. No, the value-judgment was rooted in a deeper realm, in a dictum that goes all the way back to the God of Abraham, Isaac, and Jacob—the Creator's declaration that persons are more valuable than things. In a hierarchy of values that is older than Sinai, this fundamental thesis underlines the influence of religious vision on practical behavior.

In our own century we have seen a graphic illustration in the history of the Third Reich. In the 1930s there came to power a group of Germans who did not accept this ancient vision of reality, and we well know the havoc that resulted from such a shift in perception. In one parable Jesus described an unjust judge as "neither fearing God nor having regard for man," and these two characteristics inevitably are linked in actual practice. "Where there is no God, eventually there will be no man," Helmut Thielicke observed grimly after living through the Nazi era. The crucial dimension in Christian ethics is reached by opening our eyes to all that exists in other human beings. Because we emanate from the same Source, we are then able to see the commonality that does exist; our differences cease to be threatening and become instead the bases for creativity.

This way to see and relate to human diversity was brought home to me by Morton Kelsey's essay on one of the great pastoral challenges of our time—ministry to the homosexual. Three explanations have been

n homosexual

offered concerning that condition, Kelsey says. Some maintain that the cause is physiological—that certain human beings are simply born different, and therefore homosexuality is more like being left-handed in a right-handed culture than anything else, and should be so regarded. We do not condemn a person for being born a certain way.

Another school of thought regards homosexuality as largely the result of cultural rebellion. Since heterosexuality has been the predominant mode of behavior across the years, there are certain defiant types who say, "I am going to be different." These people choose an alternative way in order to prove their individuality.

The third interpretation sees homosexuality as a matter of arrested development. All of us begin our pilgrimages of personhood in a narcissistic state—that is, we are largely preoccupied with ourselves—and then we move into what Kelsey calls mirror relationships, a time when little boys prefer to be with little boys and little girls with little girls. That is the easiest way, Kelsey says, to begin to step outside ourselves and explore the fuller dimensions of our own uniqueness. The third step in normal developmental growth, however, comes when we venture on to interact with those unlike ourselves. Of course, in sexual terms, this would mean heterosexual relationships. Somehow, says Kelsey, the homosexual becomes stuck in the middle stage. For some reason, these individuals can tolerate only mirror relationships.

But Kelsey does not stop there. "It needs to be pointed out," he goes on, "that homosexuality is not the only manifestation of arrested development.

Racial prejudice, religious bigotry, and ideological fanaticism are also expressions of the same thing. In each case, there is an inability to tolerate the not-like-one's-self. There is the obsession to stay only with one's own kind and have nothing to do with diversity."

When I read that passage, its impact was so powerful that I put the book down to think. Suddenly things began to connect that had never connected before. To be honest, while I had never been condemning of that particular human condition, I had never until that moment been able fully to empathize with the homosexual; I had never been physically attracted to another of my own sex. But while I had not had that experience, God knows that I had had trouble relating to people of a different color or different ideas or different sorts of behavior!

Now, for the first time, I was able to say "we" instead of "you" to that condition and to realize again a truth I had forgotten—that differences between humans are more a matter of degree than of kind. We all have so much in common: We are all stuck at some point in the pilgrimage from narcissism to mirror relationships to interactions with those who are not like ourselves. When it is stated like that, who can claim to be full-grown and complete? We all have our "antipathy people," people who represent all that frightens and repulses us. Yet the whole thrust of the gospel is toward maturity, and what is maturity, if not learning to interact with all kinds of diversity?

Jesus said very clearly, "If ye love those which love you, what reward have ye?" He taught that the real way to growth lies in loving your enemy. What did

Jesus mean? Think about it for a moment—who is an enemy if not someone who is so unlike us that we find that person distasteful or threatening? And yet the truth is that we grow in this life through interaction with those who are not like ourselves. There is a law written deep in the order of things: *Sameness makes for sterility; diversity makes for creativity.* At the sexual level, when two who are not alike come together in intimacy, new life is born. At the intellectual level, when one puts oneself in touch with a person who knows something one does not know, new knowledge is possible. Jesus' statement "If ye love those which love you, what reward have ye?" could translate, "If you stay cloistered in mirror relationships, what enlargement or growth is possible?" Diversity is essential to the creative process.

But then the question arises, Where do we find the courage to venture out to those who are not like ourselves? It comes, I think, from the kind of vision that sees others with the eyes of the heart. This vision sets in motion the process that can reverse the tragedy of the two knights by allowing us to become aware of what already is. Other people are our brothers and sisters by nature because we all originated from the same Source. And to see others in that way is the secret to the reconciling process.

I have long loved a certain episode in II Kings. While the prophet Elisha was in Dothan, the Syrian army slipped in by night to capture him. When his young servant woke up early the next morning and saw the enemy encamped on every side, he dissolved in panic and rushed to tell the prophet the bad news. However, the old man of God responded very calmly:

*story in
II Kings*
good

"Fear not, for they that be with us are more than they that be with them." Then, significantly, Elisha dropped to his knees and prayed that the Lord would open the eyes of the young man so that he could see things as they really were. And when the young man looked again, behold, around the forces of the Syrians were the horses and chariots of God—as far as he could see!

ch's Task

The situation that faced Elisha is like the one that faces the church today. The church's task is to open people's eyes to what already is, but has not yet been recognized. When that task is accomplished, the redemptive and creative power to relate to "significantly other" others will follow.

9

Caring for the Whole Creation

I did not grow up in a church that emphasized social justice or concern for corporate issues. My Southern Baptist tradition was largely individualistic and pietistic in its focus. I realize now that there is a historical basis for this attitude—our roots lie at one of the lower rungs of the social-class ladder. Southern Baptists were largely rural folk, and tenant farmers, at that. They did not own much property or possess a great deal of political or social power. Therefore they realistically focused their attention on those sectors of human experience over which they did have some control—their sexual organs (Thou shall not commit adultery), their tongues (Thou shall not take the name of the Lord thy God in vain), their mouths (Thou shall not drink liquor), and their hands (Thou shall not steal). The larger issues of public justice and economic policies lay beyond their influence, so they developed largely as an apolitical group, as far as altering the structures of society was concerned.

But those Baptist tenant farmers gradually experienced great upward mobility, and the result is that today their grandsons and great-grandsons sit on city councils and corporate boards, and even help to govern the nation (Jimmy Carter is a Southern Baptist). Sadly, many of these politically and economically potent individuals still view morality solely in pietistic and individualistic terms. They fail to relate their religion to the corporate decision making that affects whole communities. My particular religious group badly needs to catch up in this area; it needs to develop a religious and moral maturity comparable to the power many now hold.

In a real sense, however, this challenge is akin to the one that faces the whole church in the 1980s. While some denominations have had more experience in social involvement than others, has any part of the church a right to be complacent? We all have much growing to do to become effective in facilitating social justice and creating a more humane society. The challenge to move from self-concern to planetary responsibility is awesome, perhaps the most demanding and difficult of all. Because I was given so little early training in this area of growth, I have had to begin from scratch, but that is all the more reason to see this challenge as the exciting one it is.

The thread that ties this whole book together is as foundational in this area, however, as in the others. As we seek to become protectors and nourishers and fulfillers—not only of structures of society but of the whole creation—we need not import something foreign. Once again, our task is to open blind eyes to the capacity that already exists within every human being, to expand what is inherent within each of us to wider and wider areas of concern.

I once knew a very wealthy man in the Deep South who owned row on row of cheap rental property, inhabited largely by low-income black families. When a local housing-code ordinance was passed, requiring that indoor plumbing be installed in those dwellings, the man was greatly incensed and railed against the "do-gooders" and "communists" who were behind this drive for improvement. When significant figures were presented to document the number of children who had suffered from diptheria and other diseases caused by inadequate water sources and poor sewage disposal in those houses, the landlord was unmoved.

But shortly afterward, that man's own beloved grandson became critically ill and was rushed to the hospital. I was called as one of the ministers to be with the family, and I shall never forget that grandfather's intense concern. "No expense must be spared," he said as he nervously paced the hospital corridor.

I remember pondering this baffling paradox on my way home: How can a person be so concerned for the plight of one child and, at the same time, be so unconcerned about the plight of other children? I faced a crucial option that night in relation to our human situation—I could feel rage and despair in the face of such a glaring contradiction, or I could take heart from the fact that the impulse to care for and nurture another does exist embryonically in the human makeup. I chose then, and I continue to choose the way of hope—we must work incessantly to

selectivity of our concerns

fan that tiny flame of concern until it becomes more and more inclusive, until it finally embraces the whole of creation.

morality + *number*

I once heard a mathematical definition of morality: The fewer persons you are concerned about as you consider what to do with your power, the less moral an action is; the more people you take into consideration as you consider the impact of your action, the more moral it becomes. The thieves who shamelessly robbed the man going from Jerusalem to Jericho in Jesus' famous parable of the good Samaritan represent one end of the continuum. They cared only for themselves and used their power without regard for the harm it did others. At the other end of the continuum is God himself, as described in John 3:16: "For God so loved the world, that he gave his only begotten Son." Here God is taking the whole of creation into account in the exercise of power. Such a definition of morality points us toward the goal of an ever-widening, increasingly inclusive circle of responsible action.

It is often noted that the technological advances of the twentieth century have shrunk our planet to the size of a global village. Our ability to travel faster than sound and to become aware almost instantly of worldwide events has rendered provincialism obsolete. We all need to become "planetary" in terms of awareness and responsibility. We have in us the capacity to care; the challenge is to enlarge that capacity to include "the many."

A priest in Graham Greene's famous novel *The Power and the Glory* had sired an illegitimate child whom he came to love very much. He struggled, of

the priest in novel

course, with many conflicting emotions. But as he was about to part from his daughter one day, he said to himself, "One must come to love every soul as if it were one's own child. . . . The passion to protect must extend itself over the whole world." That attitude should be our goal, it seems to me. The seed is already present. It needs only to be nourished to bring forth genuine revolutionary activity in behalf of our entire planet.

That term *revolutionary* is admittedly a very ambiguous one. I recall that in the 1960s, I followed with keen interest a debate in theological circles as to whether Jesus could be classified as a revolutionary. It seems obvious that he was not officially aligned with the most prominent revolutionary movement of his day, the Jewish Zealots, who were determined to overthrow Rome no matter what the method. Perhaps Jesus had good reason to avoid such identification. The Gospels give abundant evidence that he had contact with representatives of the movement. In fact, some of his own disciples had been Zealots. Yet Jesus must have realized that the Zealots had succumbed to the temptation that is always present in that kind of endeavor: They had taken on the very characteristics that they initially had set out to oppose.

The trouble with so many political revolutions, observed G. K. Chesterton, is that they tend to revolve. When the oppressed set out to overthrow the oppressor, there is often genuine moral outrage at flagrant misuse of power. But in an effort to oust the rascals, it is easy to adopt the same methods. When the underdogs finally prove successful, they often have become so like the oppressors that there is no longer any essential difference between the two groups. The Quakers have a saying: "If, in order to defeat the beast, one must become a beast, then beastiality has in fact won." The great temptation in all revolutionary movements is to degenerate into a mirror image of the very injustices one has set out to correct. My feeling is that this happened to the Zealot movement in the first century and thus Jesus chose not to cast his lot with them.

However, Jesus actually may have been one of the greatest revolutionaries who ever lived, in the sense that he was amazingly effective in calling powerless people to an awareness of their potency! He was successful in motivating thousands of Jewish peasants and working people to realize that they need not be as apathetic as they had chosen to be. Jesus began his ministry on this resounding note of challenge: "The time is fulfilled, and the kingdom of God is at hand: repent . . . and believe the gospel." I think he was challenging those people to repent of their impotence and to begin to exercise the power they already possessed. Certainly his influence on Simon Peter is worthy of the adjective *revolutionary*.

Christ should be our model and inspiration as we extend our areas of responsibility farther and farther in the decade of the 1980s. It is the church's task to make people more aware of their potential and of the options that are open to them. Most of us are not the victims we have imaged ourselves to be. We have too quickly acquiesced to the belief that "there is nothing we can do." All Christians should be involved in the vision of the revolutionary Jesus, the vision that came alive for ordinary people—the challenge to move from "I am" to "I can" to "I will."

Whether or not to identify with the more structured revolutionary groups of our time is a matter for each individual to decide. However, to join what Albert Camus called the Humane Revolution, a revolution which attempts to put an end to over/under structures altogether, is to express the essence of Christianity.

In what specific areas should the church exercise this revolutionary concern and activity? The list is endless. But three problems are, I believe, among the most pressing.

The first is the age-old dilemma of *economic justice.* How can the material goods of this world be fairly distributed among the members of the human family? Decades ago, Ghandi observed that there are sufficient material resources on this planet for everyone's need, but not enough for everyone's greed. The question with which we all will need to struggle is a simple one: How much is enough? A small proportion of the inhabitants of this planet has cornered most of its economic resources. And while those people attempt to protect what they have and amass more, a greater proportion does not possess enough to survive. I do not have the expertise to lay out a blueprint for the correction of this oldest of human problems, but I do feel that its overarching cause is fear. Unless the church can effectively deal with this primal reality, not much societal change will take place.

I have been greatly influenced at this point by Langdon Gilkey's *Shantung Compound,* his reflections on three years in a Japanese internment camp during

World War II. Gilkey was educated in the liberal tradition dominant at Harvard in the 1930s, and when he began his work in a preparatory school in China, he was convinced that in order to foster responsible behavior, one need only teach people right from wrong.

The Japanese were at war with the Chinese during those years, and after Pearl Harbor, they placed all Allied citizens in internment camps. Gilkey was sent to a former Presbyterian mission in the coastal province of Shantung. The living space was cramped, the food supply unpredictable, and the future uncertain. Gilkey was astonished that the pervading fear and insecurity which haunted some 1,500 American, Canadian, British, and European citizens—most of them highly educated and socially sensitive—could turn even missionaries into raging survivalists. When it was a matter of their own welfare or that of their children, those individuals lost all concern for the common good.

A dramatic example occurred when the American Red Cross succeeded in sending 2,100 food parcels into the compound. The authorities decreed that each prisoner would receive one parcel, and because the shipment had come from their country, the Americans could share the remainder. When this decision was announced, the Americans caucused and formally protested. They proposed that each of the 300 Americans should receive seven packets and that the remaining 1,200 prisoners should receive none!

This experience permanently altered Gilkey's moral understanding: It taught him that the need for security is a formative reality. There are finally two poles, it seems—love and fear—and each has the power to negate the other. "Perfect love has the power to cast out fear," said John. The reverse is also true: Fear certainly has the power to cast out love.

I feel that the church must take this vision of reality into careful consideration if we are to make significant progress toward greater economic justice. The security of individuals in their own relationship to the Ultimate is not an irrelevant issue if we wish the world's population to become more generous and less acquisitive. When one understands that "he who gave us the good old days can be trusted to give us good new days," the possibility of becoming a generous sharer rather than a frightened animal is much more likely. The dynamic that led members of the early Christian community "to hold all things in common" undoubtedly resulted from the security that they came to feel— security in God's care and in the care of one another. What strategies can the church devise to enable each of us to ask, How much is enough?—in relation not only to our own needs, but to the needs of other human beings? A genuine concern for this issue is certainly not all that is called for here, but it is a beginning.

A second area of challenge has to do with the *racial and sexist discrimination* that has so plagued our human experience. My late mentor, Carlyle Marney, used to say that we have confused "the adjectives and nouns of life." *Black* and *white*, *male* and *female*, *rich* and *poor*—all are adjectives, he contended. That is, these words are descriptive of certain facets of a human being, but in no case do they constitute total definitions. *Human being, person*—these are the proper nouns in authentic vocabulary. Most of us still have "miles to go" before we will be able to allow a person's gender or skin color to function solely in an adjectival way. Though I like this way of defining the issue, I realize that far more is needed than simply a fresh way to describe the situation. Patterns of racial discrimination are so rooted in custom, history, and economics, and are so full of our own projected shadows that we must make an effort to recognize their distorting effect on our perceptions and our actions.

The Gender Revolution, too, calls for changes in our perception and behavior. We must remember that change, by its very nature, represents gain as well as loss. In the midst of turmoil, we tend to focus only on what we must give up, overlooking what we will receive. There will be tremendous benefits, in time, for both males and females as every woman receives that which long has been given to every man—respect, pay commensurate with work, a voice in determining individual destiny, access to authority and power; and when we expect of every woman that which long has been expected of every man—responsible action, concern for truth, compassion for other human beings, commitment to the common good. What tremendous giftedness and creativity will be released!

I heard Leontyne Price sing at the inauguration of Governor William Winter of Mississippi. As a child in Laurel, Mississippi, she had been identified as having prodigious talent and was given the opportunity to become a magnificent musician. I could not help thinking of the many other fantastic human gifts that have lived and died in black bodies in the South, with no one ever sensing such potential because the adjective *black* had been elevated to the role of a noun.

When I heard a magnificent young woman preach
at the summer institute of the Princeton Theological
Seminary, I felt that the art of preaching had never
been exercised more powerfully. Again, I wondered *woman*
how many preaching gifts have lived and died in *preacher*
female bodies because the church had allowed
adjectives to function in a nominative sense. For all the
readjustment such changes will entail, the benefit for
all society is immeasurable.

To the same grammatical issue, I would add the
growing preoccupation with athletic prowess. Herb
Barks, president of The Baylor School in Chatta- *sports*
nooga, recently gave a very insightful talk on the way
this overemphasis has affected the value system of the
whole nation. The ability to pass a football or shoot a
basketball, he said, really is adjectival and not
nominative. Our culture, however, has come to
reward these particular talents in a manner out of all
proportion to moral, intellectual, or aesthetic ability.
"No college president ever arrives in a Lear jet to ask
me, 'Where is your best student leader?' or to say,
'Show me the young person who has the greatest
capacity to become an energizer for the future,'" said
Barks. "No, it is the coaches with their incredibly
lucrative offers who come. And they give our youth a
vision of values that is utterly out of touch with reality."

I think the implications of this trend are just now
becoming evident to many of us. We are placing far
too high a premium on certain activities and far too
little value on other processes—processes that are
utterly essential for the survival of our culture.
Somewhere in the span of my own adulthood, athletics
moved from a form of recreation to a national

obsession. The ethos has shifted from Grantland Rice's "It's not whether you win or lose, but how you play the game" to Vince Lombardi's "Winning is not everything—it is the only thing." I believe the whole Watergate tragedy was an expression in the political arena of this headlong passion to win at any cost. Ways must be found to direct the nation's consciousness against this particular value-judgment and its effect on all our lives.

In regard to value-judgments, then, as well as to discrimination of all kinds, the church's challenge to put adjectives and nouns in their proper places is enormous indeed.

The third, and beyond doubt the greatest challenge facing the church today and for an indeterminable time to come, is *the effort to avert the total destruction of this planet through the misuse of nuclear power.* Never before have human beings possessed such a level of potential and thus been confronted with such an awesome and final array of options. This situation represents the most demanding test of the human spirit since that moment of initial creation when, according to Simone Weil, "God ceased to be everything so we humans could become something." It was that act on God's part which set the stage for human history.

With the discovery of the power within the atom, we have moved to a point where the question To be or not to be? ceases to be a quote from Shakespeare and becomes the all-pervasive issue. Will the human spirit finally be able to use for good what the human mind has discovered and developed? In *Now and Then,* Frederick Buechner writes, "There are times when I suspect the world may come to an end before most of

us are ready for it to—which would have the
advantage at least of our not having to leave, one by
one, while the party is still going strong—but most of
the time I believe that the world will manage somehow
to survive us."

Which of those ideas will be fulfilled? With all my
heart, I opt for the latter. After all, the generations
before us, for all their faults and failings, kept the
party going until we joined it. And they fully expected
us to be as hospitable to our children as they themselves had been to us. The earth is a gift, and all that is
within it. How can our generation regard it as a
possession and arrogantly and ungratefully turn out
the lights? How dare we deprive future generations of
its joy? The very thought is repugnant to the human
spirit's sense of fairness and sanity.

However, more will be required than the vague
hope that "the world will manage somehow to survive
us." In the 1980s, millions of us must put forth much
more imagination and effort and sacrifice to discover
ways to use nuclear power creatively and safely than
was expended by a few to discover and develop it.

I, for one, see reason for hope. As I write these
words, I sense a worldwide awakening to the
implications of this situation, I recently talked to an
Episcopal bishop who reported that everywhere he
turned, there seemed to be an explosion of energies
focused on this crisis. At a meeting I attended the
other night, a veteran Roman Catholic right-to-lifer
saw the connection between her reverence-for-life
concerns and the nuclear threat. That meeting
contained a startling mixture of political opposites, but
those people, whose moral vision had been confined to

a narrowly defined area, had begun to widen their boundaries to include more and more realities. It was an illustration of the very process I have identified—an expansion of the capacity for concern that all humans possess. As I left that gathering of Pro-lifers for Survival, I felt that this might well have been a sacrament of hope—a glimpse of what is now only faintly visible on the horizon.

It is late in the day, and the stakes are obviously high, but it is not too late for all of us who care for God's creation—all of us who are enjoying the party—to act to insure its continuation. After all, we humans are not the only actors on the mysterious stage of history. There is Another who so loves this world that he has done and will do extraordinarily ingenious and surprising things to save and redeem it. And although that does not take us humans off the hook—we must collaborate with him with all our strength and with all our heart—it does make our despair for our world seem a bit presumptuous.

Who knows what we and he might still do . . . ? With eyes that are at least beginning to open after long years of blindness, I, for one, choose to make my life in hope!